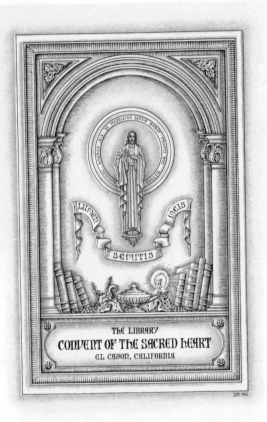

Approach to
Christian Sculpture

I. *The Last Supper* (detail)

APPROACH
TO
CHRISTIAN
SCULPTURE

by

Dom Hubert van Zeller

Sheed & Ward - New York

10303

MANUFACTURED IN THE UNITED STATES OF AMERICA

To NIALL,

BY WAY OF CROSSING HIS SWORD WITH A CHISEL

Contents

Contents

List of Illustrations

Preface

MAY I, forestalling the reviewers who will not be slow to notice its shortcomings, myself review this book? "The author"—so I would write if I were employed to review—"has clearly not read half the works which should be read before such a study is attempted; he can pretend to no more than the most elementary knowledge of aesthetics; nor has he the excuse of being a well-known sculptor from whom books may be expected in the way that paintings are expected from heads of state. What right has such an amateur, and in such a small volume, to discuss such a specialized subject?" The argument about being an amateur is never wholly convincing: every professional has been an amateur at one time. But the charges are valid. While not attempting to advance credentials I do advance an explanation. My job is religion and cutting stone. After more than a quarter of a century in both these activities I have come to see the connection between the two. Having treated elsewhere of religion, I treat here of cutting stone. The one, in my experience, has helped the other. I might add that working in company has enabled me to benefit by the ideas of others, working in solitude has enabled me to form my own. Besides, and this raises another point, I am not writing because I am qualified to discuss Christian sculpture but because I am dismayed at the present lack of direction in Christian sculpture.

It is not that interest in sacred art is altogether wanting, even in England, but that it is wanting among those who are in a position to steer its course. A number of reasons could be given for this: the clergy have already enough on their hands in the building of churches and schools without having to worry about getting the right sort of statues; the more influential laity have never had it put to them that there is any real principle involved; the artists are content to satisfy the general demand without seriously compromising their artistic consciences.[1] Thus the rest of the faithful, those who are not either ecclesiastics or benefactors or professionals, have to manage the best they can with what is given to them. So it goes on: no sure lead being given, no true standards of appreciation being learned, no wide demand for the services which an authentic artistic tradition is capable of rendering.

The problem is partly economical, therefore, and

[1] Cardinal Lercaro refers to the priests, the people, and the artists as "the three pillars of the Church's art." If pillars are to be effective in the work of support, they must agree with one another about what they are supporting.

partly cultural. While there is nothing much one can do about the economical side of it, there should be ample scope on the cultural. Before we go any further, the word "culture," as meant here, must be properly understood. It must not be taken as implying the esoteric—indeed the whole burden of the argument is that art appreciation must *not* belong only to an initiated class—but the way of current thinking. One of the main difficulties about art appreciation is, as we shall see on a later page, that while half the world imagines it to be a faculty automatically possessed by all and knowing no other standard but the subjective, the other half imagines it to be the prerogative of an exclusive few, the sophisticated. This second mistaken attitude is liable to be strengthened by the very people who are trying to break it down. It is assumed, for example, that the writings of men like Jacques Maritain, Pie Régamey, E. I. Watkin, and the late Maurice Denis are beyond the ordinary person's intelligence. "It is gratifying to know that there are Catholics who can write at that level about art" is the attitude, "but of course it is above one's head." Culture, then, is to be understood here not as cultivated thought but as the cultivation of thought. And in the cultivation of thought it is everybody's business to take a part.[2]

[2] "A book like the one Charlier has just wrtttten, *The Martyrdom of Art or Art Thrown to the Beasts* (1957), as

This book is accordingly addressed to a variety of readers. For the layman and priest alike, it is meant to clarify the issues at stake; for the stone-carver it is meant to make more precisely religious the employment of his powers; for the non-Christian it is meant to explain what our artistic tradition and sculptural effort are about. A book which proposes to itself so wide a range both of reader and of purpose will have to keep its eye on several horizons at once—technical, historical, aesthetic, religious—and so will tend to share, in its advantages as well as in its defects, the character of an empire exhibition: some of it may be of interest to many, all of it will be of interest to few. Much, whichever way you look at it, will be what Fleet Street calls "inside tack."

Also resulting from the employment of such a method must be, anyway to the reader who is an expert in any one of the fields mentioned above, the trite

---

well as similar writings by Thibon or Marcel de Corte, show with all needed clearness that this art does not exist *against* modern culture, i.e. in a total lack of sympathy with its ideals, realizations and plans, and that on the contrary it wants to develop in accordance with the idea of returning to Christian ways of working . . . it would without doubt be unjust to ignore this position, but it would be just as absurd to believe that there lie sufficient elements for a solution. We too want Christendom, but not the kind outlined or described by these writers."—Dom Frédéric Debuyst, *Art d'Eglise*, no. 105, *Expositions de 1958.*

nature of some of its conclusions. But the true very often *is* trite, and I for one am not above the use of the platitude in a good cause. One man's truism is another man's revelation. Nor does anyone have to accept my opinion—where it *is* an opinion and not a presentation of the Church's doctrine—or even respect it. This is the advantage of so much connected with the subject: there are a few fundamental truths which we must acknowledge if we are to get anywhere at all in it, and the rest is anybody's guess. Just because I happen to think that the Romanesque represents the peak of Christian sculpture, and that the Gothic Revival represents the depths, I do not demand the agreement of my readers. The most that I would ask of a reader would be the patience to note the reasons which I might advance for my view. Every book about art, as about all subjects that are worth while, is a personal book.

While the principles outlined in the following pages would apply substantially to art as a whole, they are here narrowed to the sculptural frame of reference for two reasons. First, because sculpture is the only branch of art about which I have been able to learn anything worth telling to anyone else. Second, because it is the branch which, on the authority of the most knowledgeable, most truly reflects the feeling of its age. "Sculpture sums up the main features of an epoch," writes

Sir Leigh Ashton, one-time Director of the Victoria and
Albert Museum, "and if we remain blind to its appeal,
we debar ourselves from much that is most valuable
in the creative achievement of the past."[3] "Let us not
forget," writes the Russian sculptor, Naum Gabo,
"that all the greatest epochs at the moment of their
apogee manifested their spiritual tension in sculpture."[4] It is not a question of which art-form, painting
or sculpture, is more excellent, but which art-form is
more representative. That Mardo Rosso thought sculpture more "expressive" than painting or that Leonardo
da Vinci thought painting more "intellectual" than
sculpture is not strictly to the point. More to the point
would be to claim that Rosso as a sculptor better typified the late nineteenth century than Leonardo da
Vinci as a painter typified the late fifteenth.

Further restricting the frame of reference, the subject-matter of this book envisages primarily carving,
either in wood or stone, and only to a secondary extent
modelling. Again it is not a question of which is super-
ior, carving or modelling, but of which is felt to be
the more representative. Certainly it is the more direct.
Eric Gill anyway took it to be so. "I shall assume that
the word *sculpture*," he writes in a short work which

[3] *Style in Sculpture,* p. 7.
[4] Quoted by E. H. Ramsden in *Sculpture: Theme and Variations,* p. 47.

will be much drawn upon in the course of the present study, "is the name given to the craft by which things are cut out of solid material, whether in relief or in the round. I shall not use the word as applying to the craft of modelling in clay or wax."[5] In an engraving rather extravagantly called *The Appropriate Activity of Man*, Gill shows a stone-carver at work on a statue of the Madonna and Child; it probably never entered his head to show a man painting or modelling. "The cutting of stone," says the same authority, "is the type of the craft of the sculptor. The modelling of clay is for him merely the means of making preliminary sketches . . . it is not desirable to make exact models in clay, because the sort of thing which can be easily and suitably constructed in clay may not be, and generally is not, suitable for carving in stone . . . modelling in clay is a process of addition; whereas carving is a process of subtraction."[6]

Though Gill champions the *taille directe*, and is strict in his use of the word "sculpture," he is not such an oracle that he must be followed without qualification. Rodin's suggestion, far-fetched perhaps but not without its force, is in this connection worth remembering: that when we think of God in the act of creating we think of him as modelling, not as carving. Be

[5] *Sculpture*, p. 21.
[6] *Ibid.*, pp. 26, 27.

this as it may, and allowing a margin for allusion to the kindred craft, the present work has the carving of stone principally in view.

Passing from apology and explanation to acknowledgement, I must express my grateful indebtedness to those authors living and dead whose books I have found particularly helpful in the composition of what follows. Among recent publications the four most frequently consulted are: *Art Sacré au XXe Siècle* by P. R. Régamey (Editions du Cerf, 1952); *Sculpture: Theme and Variations* by E. H. Ramsden (Lund Humphries, 1953); *A Concise History of Art* by Germain Bazin, translated by Francis Scarfe (London: Thames and Hudson, 1958; Boston [*A History of Art*]: Houghton Mifflin, 1959); *Atlas of the Early Christian World* by F. van der Meer and Christine Mohrmann, translated by Mary Hedlund and H. H. Rowley (Nelson, 1958). Less recent, but as often and as gratefully turned to, are: *Style in Sculpture* by Sir Leigh Ashton, F.S.A. (Oxford University Press, 1947); *The Sculptor Speaks*, Jacob Epstein to Arnold Haskell (Heinemann, 1931); *Some Modern Sculptors* by Stanley Casson (Oxford: Clarendon Press, 1928); and the following works by Eric Gill: *Sculpture, An Essay on Stone-cutting with a Preface about God* (St. Dominic's Press; New York, Chaucer Head, 1932), *Beauty Looks After Herself* (Sheed and Ward, 1933); *In a Strange Land*

(Jonathan Cape, 1944); *Last Essays* (Jonathan Cape, 1942). To the above must be added the following articles printed in *Modern Sacred Art,* edited by Joan Morris (Sands, 1938): *Reflections on Sacred Art* by Jacques Maritain; *Art and Society* by E. I. Watkin; *The Modern Artist and Sacred Art* by G. Severini; *The Concept of Beauty* by T. C. Terburg.

To those who have provided the photographs I am also much indebted: Mr. Desmond Tripp, A.I.B.P., F.R.P.S. (frontispiece and plates 1 to 8); Mr. John Cotton (plate 9); the Hon. Patrick Morris (plate 10); Messrs. R. A. Haines and B. Clarke (plate 12); Mr. Douglas Steuert (plate 13). The camera has shown itself to be kind to stone-cutting.

Approach to
Christian Sculpture

1. Remote

i

BEFORE a piece of sculpture can be called Christian we must be sure that it can be called sculpture. Our approach to the spiritual significance will be by way of the material substance: the sculptural principle must be got right first. Sculpture is that arrangement of interrelating planes, masses, surfaces and lines which results in a unity corresponding to a unity which exists in the sculptor's mind. It is a certain thickness shaped at the hand of man and inspired by man's creative thought. "Thickness" demanding more than surface, "hand" demanding more than machine, "thought" demanding more than visual imagination.

So if Rodin said of sculpture, as he is alleged to have said, that it was "the art of presenting to the eye the travelling outline," he cannot have meant to account for more than one aspect of the art—and that not the most important.[1] As they stand, the words suggest that

[1] A more profound definition, and one which is certainly authentic, is Rodin's statement that a piece of sculpture is "a

all the sculptor has to do is to see that when you walk round his work you can trace an interesting edge to it. But Rodin would have stoutly denied this idea—with its implication of a revolving silhouette. More important than the perimeter is the volume which comes bulging out at you between the outlines. Unless this thickness curves away interestingly and convincingly towards the outlines, the piece of carving will be at best only a drawing transferred from one medium to another.

Even in the case of a relief, where outlines have a direct bearing upon the composition, the essential quality does not lie in the boundary but in what stands out between the boundaries. A relief is not a drawing conceived in depth. A relief, just as much as a carving in the round, is first of all a thing of depth. A relief is a piece of sculpture which happens to have an outline fixed in a certain place. Its outline does not travel all the way. A relief should be thought of as a statue which stops short at a particular stage and does not go round at the back.

Height and width can be planned beforehand; they can be measured out on paper; they constitute what is called (rather inadequately) the design. The quality

---

drawing from every angle." The two pronouncements are just enough alike to suggest that there was in fact only one, and that "un dessein de toutes les côtés" has been misquoted.

of thickness, however, is more elusive. Its effect in the finished work cannot be so precisely foretold. But it is this quality, which in the craft they call "roundness," that makes sculpture. The sculptor who can foresee his planes and surfaces, who can judge beforehand the roundness which will come out of his composition, and who over and above has a thought to convey, truly has in his head a design. Otherwise he has only got a pattern.

So whether working in the round or in relief, the sculptor must think in terms of the third dimension every bit as much as he must think in terms of the other two. It is in the substance of the work that the substance of the thought is primarily conveyed. While Maillol's "roundness is all" may be an exaggeration, it is not much of an exaggeration. As an example of roundness, from a more recent inspiration than Maillol's but carrying the same doctrine along its logical course, there is the work of Mr. Henry Moore. For Henry Moore, as for Jean Arp, Barbara Hepworth, Guito Knoop, and a number of other contemporary sculptors, roundness is of the essence of sculptural expression.

But you do not have to go all the way to abstract or near-abstract carving in order to see what roundness means to sculpture. The *Venus of Willendorf* in Vienna and the *Venus of Lespugue* at Saint-Germain show that roundness was the first consideration during the

Approach to Christian Sculpture

Upper Palaeolithic Period.[2] The same quality is evident
during the best periods of Greek carving, and in the
truest examples of sculpture that have come since.
You see it in every work of Michelangelo, Rodin, Ber-
nard, Gaudier-Brzeska, Gordine; you see it in much
of the work of Epstein, Mestrovic, and Gill.[3] The first
thing to look for in sculpture is not skilfulness of execution, not resemblance to corresponding objects in nature, not usefulness. The first thing to look for (leaving
the question of interior actuations until later) is the
shape of the thing in bulk.

It would be a mistake to infer from this that the best
sculpture must be the *thickest* sculpture, and that the
sculptor's job is to turn out good solid stuff which could
never be mistaken for whatever it was that served as
model. There is much thick sculpture in London which
is not at all good sculpture: the lions in Trafalgar
Square, for instance. Just as in painting it is a question
not of the strongest colours but of the right colours,
so in sculpture it is a question not of weight but of
balance. Where everything in a piece of sculpture is

[2] So not later than 5000 B.C. and possibly as early as 7000 B.C.
For illustrations see Bazin, *A Concise History of Art*, p. 14, and
Sir Kenneth Clark's *The Nude*, pp. 64, 65.

[3] Nowhere in Gill's work is this quality more apparent than
in the *Prospero and Ariel* group which stands above the en-
trance to Broadcasting House. Prospero's knee and the whole
of the Ariel figure would satisfy Maillol at his most exacting.

integrated and proportionate, the dimensions are of secondary consequence. Where the thicknesses are related to one another the effect will be one of lightness. In the grounds at the back of New York's Museum of Modern Art lies a huge recumbent figure by Maillol. Though enormous, it does not give the impression of being massive. You feel that if you pushed it in the right place you could tip it over with a finger into the ornamental sheet of water at its side. Only when you have stopped to think do you realize that to budge it an inch you would need a crane.

The sense of heaviness is normally a weakness rather than a strength. When the monumental *looks* monumental, there is usually something wrong with it. Ernst Barlach, surely one of the finest sculptors of our time, often lends a feeling of heaviness to his figures; but this is deliberate, and in order to express clumsiness. Carl Milles, when he wants to expose the materialism of the age, does the same. Heaviness is all right as a device; it is disastrous as a mistake.

ii

But there are other points to be noted in the execution of the sculptor's idea than those of relating the masses, preserving the line, and suggesting depths. A cardinal requirement, and one which is made much of in any discussion of the subject, is truth. Truth is essentially the same in sculpture as it is in anything else, but there are in sculpture certain applications of it which need indicating. If truth is conformity to a standard, there will be in every art certain canons, conventions, principles, which are proper to that art and to which works of that art must be referred. If the works fail to conform, they are not expressions of that art but rebels against it. Whether carved, modelled, written, painted, danced, acted, or picked out on a musical instrument, the work must correspond both with the conception in the artist's mind and with the medium chosen for the job.

In sculpture the relationship between the sculptor and his material is as important as the relationship is in religion between God and man. In each case the relationship rests upon the fidelity of the human being to an existing law. The realization of truth is measured by the degree of conformity to the particular standard set. The inspiration which animates both the sculptor and the Christian has to find its appropriate expression through the right handling of the right medium. In the case of Christianity the inspiration is Christ and his Gospel, in the case of sculpture it is whatever the sculptor chooses to allow; in the case of Christianity the medium is life, in the case of sculpture it is whatever his hands are fashioning.

So the actual execution of the work can be seen as

the development both of the sculptor's inspiration and the material's possibility. It is therefore up to the sculptor to choose those materials which, first as vehicles of his inspiration and second as subjects to his ability, he can best develop. "It is obvious that if you do not care in what material your idea takes shape," says Gill, "you might as well be a modeller as anything else. But if you are that kind of workman who finds in his material a complement to himself, and that material is stone, modelling in clay must be kept in a wholly subordinate position."[4] If you opt for clay you must keep the rules of clay, if you opt for stone you obey the principles of stone.

"The proper modelling of clay," says Gill earlier in the same essay, "results, and should so result, in a certain spareness and tenseness of form and any desired amount of freedom or detachment of parts. The proper carving of stone upon the other hand results, and should so result, in a certain roundness and solidity of form with no detachment of parts."[5] If Rodin's work in bronze shows the tenseness, spareness, and freedom of parts required of modelling, Gill's own achievements in stone bear out the other list's demand. As good a test as any of carved sculpture is that it should remain substantially the same after being kicked down

[4] *Sculpture,* p. 32.
[5] *Ibid.,* p. 27.

a hill as before. The test is reputed to have come from Michelangelo, and is cited here to illustrate the closeness, the self-contained character, of good carving. A modelled work of sculpture, under no such obligation to be compact, would never reach the bottom of the hill: the knees and elbows would stick in the ground.

So the manner of carving is to a certain extent governed by the matter: the chisel carves stone in one way and wood in another. Even the design is to a certain extent governed by the material used. An ivory figure is conceived in one way, a granite figure in another. The same is true of modelling: ceramics, for example, impose a whole category of precautions which can be ignored by the man who works in unglazed clay. Thus it should be possible to tell from the drawing of a statue not only whether it has been carved or modelled, but what was the substance cut or modelled. On this showing it will be noticed that my stone relief *Blessed Oliver Plunkett* (plate XI) is bad sculpture; it might equally well have been carved in wood. When a commercial firm offers to turn out a model in any one of a variety of different materials, two things can be assumed without doubt: first that the commercial firm has no sense of craft, and second that the original model is untrue to the medium of its composition.

There are, it is true, master sculptors who can rise above the laws of their medium, but to do this is the privilege of the elect. A Belloc or a Winston Churchill can take liberties with the rules laid down in Fowler: Fowler is for the ordinary man, for the careful man, for the perfectionist. A Michelangelo or a Mestrovic can override the strictest art-school rules—witness Michelangelo's *Slave* and Mestrovic's *Moses,* where in each case the marble has been forced to produce a member which stretches out into space. Certainly the Greeks did not scruple—as the *Winged Victory* of Samothrace and the *Dying Warrior* from the Temple of Aphaia show—to waive the accepted canons when it suited them.[6]

More important than fidelity to one's material is fidelity to oneself. While Michelangelo may do things with marble which marble might have every right to resent, he would never do with *Michelangelo* what his own proper genius would resent. While Mestrovic conjures out of the material new possibilities, he never strains his own possibility to a performance which is not his own. For Mestrovic to express himself in the manner of Moore would not be to express himself: it would be to do violence to himself and to truth.[7] The

[6] About a third of the *Winged Victory* is extended away from the body, and between various parts of the *Dying Warrior's* body, shield, and helmet, daylight can be seen in seven places.

[7] "Mestrovic is the only sculptor of modern times whose genesis owes little or nothing to prevailing tendencies in art

sculptor who produces works which do not express himself but someone else is making use not of a creative but of an imitative gift.

For sculpture to be alive it must emerge out of the living thought; it is dead if it follows a formula. One man may legitimately shape his thought according to the thought of another. This is what we all do when we try to follow Christ—or when we try to follow anyone who can show us the mind of Christ—but it is a mistake for a man to shape his work according to the work of another. Such a work, which is meant to be judged as a sculptural creation, can never come to life. It can survive as an example of a particular school but it cannot survive as an entity of its own.

For a style of carving to be copied, its inspiration has to be experienced. For a particular work to be copied, its original impulse must be shared; the reproduction is then not so much a copy as the expression of a similar impulse. But this is no excuse for working to another man's pattern. In my own case I learned much from my failure to model myself, in design and technique, upon the carving of Ivan Mestrovic. The purpose seemed to me logical enough: Mestrovic appeared to me to be the finest religious sculptor of the century, perhaps of any century, so I could not go wrong in

or to other masters. He is at heart the product of a natural setting and its latent traditions."—Casson, *Some Modern Sculptors*, p. 62.

slavishly following him.[8] Analysing the results of this experiment, I found that they were stone dead.

So it is no good trying to work out one's own problem according to another man's solution. Truth appears to us in its way, and we respond to it in ours. Truth remains absolute, showing itself in different degrees of clarity to different people; the response is various, showing itself variously according to individual natures. While there is no harm in following one school of sculpture rather than another, there is harm in following one school so closely that the individual creative spark is smothered. More will be said about the sculptor's personal responsibility when we come to examine his conscience towards the end of the book. What we are considering here is not so much the sculptor as the works which he produces.

So far, then, the conclusion amounts to this: carvings which are either not of the material's nature or not of the carver's nature, but are of some nature extrinsic to the relationship between material and carver, stand self-condemned.

iii

If each material has its own proper nature, so also has each art-form its own proper nature. If there are

[8] For what it is worth, it is still my opinion that Mestrovic is the finest religious sculptor of this, and perhaps of any, century.

33

reasons why works of stone may not be expressed in a way which belongs to bronze, there are much stronger reasons why sculpture may not be expressed in ways which belong to literature, drama, music and the rest. Sculpture may illustrate literature, but not do the work of literature. Sculpture may allow a certain dramatic appeal, but it may not try to do what the drama does. Sculpture must stand on its own feet and be judged in its own terms.

This means that before sculpture can serve a cause it must be justified on merits irrespective of the cause. Before it can preach a sermon or tell a story, it must prove that it has a sculptural right to raise its voice. Only when its sculptural credentials have been verified can a carving begin to think about edifying, instructing, appealing, amusing, surprising, or whatever it is that calls. A judge may make entertaining comments in court, and increase his reputation for wisdom thereby, but his value to the law will depend on his justice, not on his jokes.

Failure to grasp this essential principle about sculpture, namely that it is to be true sculpture if it is to launch out into being religious sculpture, can set off a whole train of misconceptions. Almost all the fallacies about religious art arise out of the initial fallacy which makes "what people want" the primary, and often the sole, criterion. If what people want of religion itself can be one or other of religion's secondary expressions—for example, pleasant music, intelligent sermons, spectacular ceremonies—it is not surprising that the demands which they make of religious art are also misplaced. It is the same law which holds good in either case: religion is looked to primarily for its intrinsic truth; so also is art. What is wanted *as well* as intrinsic truth is another matter.

Thus (before we get on to religious art proper) it would be extrinsic to the nature of sculpture that it should be made to jump about or recite poetry. Art-forms may be related but they do not easily mix. The only art-forms which seem able to get on with one another in each other's world are music and drama and dance. Certainly when music is introduced to sculpture —as when the statue of Amenophis at Thebes was so constructed that it gave out a scale of notes on being struck by the rays of the rising sun, or when the figure of our Lady of Lourdes plays the Lourdes hymn when lifted into the air—the result is faintly ridiculous. Ingenuity, no less than incongruity, can be one of art's worst enemies.

Sculpture, perhaps more than any other art-form, relies on unity. For sculptural coherence there must be completeness of matter as well as of thought. Extraneous material can be as disturbing to the essential entity as extraneous ideas and mannerisms. One reason why much of our modern abstract sculpture is felt to be ambiguous is surely because elements are introduced which have the effect of dividing the essential interest. While the use of string and wire in compositions which have stone or wood as their medium may well serve secondary purposes, they tend to distract from the *wholeness* of the work.

If contemporary sculpture has to meet the charge of mixing its materials, so also has the sculpture of other ages. The inlaying of various metals has been known to stone since at least the ninth century B.C. Egypt, Assyria, Chaldea, Persia and Crete passed on the tradition to the Greeks and Romans, who used the technique more sparingly. Byzantium went in for plastering its icons with precious stones, and encasing its figures in gold. But where this can be justified on the grounds that hard substances were being mixed with hard substances there is less excuse for later developments which saw the mixture of hard with soft. How are we to judge the dressed-up statues of Spain, Portugal, Latin America—and later of Italy and France? How are we to judge Degas' exquisite bronze dancers with their ballet skirts of calico?

Then there is the question of paint. For four thousand years sculptors have been painting their statues,[9]

[9] The best and most accessible of carvings which go as far back as this, and which still show signs of paint, come from

and they are not likely to stop because of anything that is said here. The *Virgins of the Acropolis,* the first of which was carved in about 550 B.C.,[10] were painted, and Plato in his *Republic* tells how the practice of painting statues was current in his time. The *Head of a Persian* from the Alexander Sarcophagus shows that however perfect the carving, and this is the best that the school of Lysippos can produce, colour was accepted as part of the composition.[11] And it is the same story all down the line: Byzantine, Romanesque, Gothic, Renaissance, Baroque, Neo-Classical (though not so much), Realist, Romantic, Neo-Primitive, and much of the carving of the present day. Abstract sculpture, though partial to other finishes and accessories, does not greatly favour paint.

So those would be counted strict who denied absolutely the right of stone to paint. But since it is after

---

Egypt. *Head of a Scribe* is given the probable date of 2400 B.C. *Head of a Queen* is placed at 1360 B.C. Both are in Paris.

[10] "This statue, which is a little less than life-size, is in many ways the most beautiful of all the series of lovely maidens of the Acropolis . . . the hair, eyes, and lips are lightly painted, the hair reddish-brown, the iris of the eye and the lips in dull red. The embroidery of the garment is picked out in blue-green. Ear-rings, probably in gold, were in the ears."—Casson, *op. cit.,* p. 26.

[11] "The eyes are brown and the oriental head-dress purple. Other figures on the relief have garments on which bright blue, yellow, and crimson are used."—*Ibid.,* p. 26.

37

all only a form of make-up, the use of paint should allow itself to be governed by a principle. The principle submitted here, for what it is worth, is a simple one: so long as paint brings out the quality of the carving it may be used; if it makes you forget the carving it may not. Sculpture is something more than a pleasing arrangement of colours produced in depths. Michelangelo's famous axiom is here most apt: "Painting is excellent in proportion as it approaches relief, and relief is bad in proportion as it partakes of the character of a picture."

The accretions mentioned up till now have all been more or less in keeping with the static character of sculpture. A problem arises in the case of modern abstract sculpture: how do the suspended, flexible, transparent, and mobile elements in free sculpture accord with the idea that sculpture is something still, fixed, solid, set? Admittedly the works of such moderns as Lynn Chadwick (using wood and stretched rayon), Alexander Calder (wire and metal), Naum Gabo (plastic and crystalline), Anton Pevsner (oxidized brass and plastic) have loosened up the older tradition. But the question turns on what may legitimately be sacrificed to the good of loosening up.

These free and mobile compositions challenge conventions which have been sacred to sculpture since before the Sphinx was planted in the desert. Indeed it might be said that the Sphinx represents a tradition of "tight" carving in which the Assyrian winged bull (no daylight showing *there* in the gaps), the Egyptian athlete (arms rigid against his sides), the Parthian noble (trousers as ample as our modern waders), the Buddha of the fourth and fifth centuries (virtually immovable) find kinship. In the same family are Barlach, Milles, Epstein today. To abandon the solid for the transparent, the rooted for what can be stirred by blowing at it, would seem to deny the nature of sculpture. Sculpture is not meant to float in the air any more than it is meant to float on the sea. What may be true decoration or true entertainment is not necessarily true sculpture. Sculpture is formidable or it is nothing.

It is difficult to see where the abstract sculptors would draw the line. If they allow as sculpture linear constructions which wave about, they should allow as sculpture the plastic model of the Holy Father which, on the release of a lever, raises the right hand and gives a triple blessing. If we, the old-fashioned traditionalists, make no claim for the clockwork Holy Father and the musical-box Lourdes figure beyond that of devotion— make no claim for the scale-playing statue of Amenophis beyond that of expertise and symbolism[12]—then

[12] The subject symbolized is the greeting between mother and son at break of day. Amenophis (or Memnon, from the Egyptian *mei-amun*, beloved of Ammon) was the Ethiopian

why should not votaries of the abstract, disclaiming sculptural pretensions, be ready to accept the label of decoration?

iv

If it is to qualify as sculpture, religious or monumental, or simply as fine art which serves no purpose beyond that of being beautiful, a work must satisfy two further conditions. But since both these arise out of the conditions which we have been considering, and are in any case obvious, they can be treated briefly. Other and more specific requirements will be considered when sculpture is surveyed in its religious context.

A carving, to be a work of true sculpture, must be proportioned. Proportioned, that is, within its borders. (What the carving must be proportioned *to* will be dealt with under the heading of "congruity.") Granted that in every work of sculpture there will be some features which have to be emphasized more than others, the need for order remains fundamental. Neither beauty nor truth can exist where there is no order.

---

prince who fought for his uncle Priam, and was killed by Achilles. His mother Eos used to weep for him before the dawn, and as the sun rose each morning the dead hero would acknowledge with the sound of gently plucked chords the tribute to his memory. Hence, though obliquely, Darwin's line: "Memnon bending o'er his broken lyre."

Where the parts are disordered, are out of proportion, the whole can be neither beautiful nor true.

Nothing shows up the false in sculpture so readily as unwarranted distortion. If the balance both of parts and of truth is to be maintained in a carving, there must be no distortion for distortion's sake. Distortion is meant to serve a purpose; it is not meant to become itself a purpose. Where the principle of distortion is misunderstood, or deliberately violated, the result is deformity. It is easy to detect in a man's work (though not so easy to detect in one's own) the straining after effect which disqualifies the carving as true sculpture. Somewhere the proportions have been neglected, the balance has been thrown out.

"A man is an artist," says Epstein, "because he has the necessary judgment and skill to know what accentuation is necessary."[13] This observation exactly states the case for legitimate distortion. The true artist measures the margin of distortion and does not step outside it. This is because he has truth as his standard. The false artist, who has not got truth as his standard, sees distortion as an excuse for affectation; for him the margin widens indefinitely.

A carving in which there is no distortion at all would be dead. It would be a mathematical rendering, an exact replica; it would have no character whatever.

[13] *The Sculptor Speaks*, p. 67.

A certain element of inexactitude is necessary to the work of translation, or the thing is not a translation but a facsimile. It is the inexactitude, controlled and according to principle, that reveals the life. The question is where to be exact and where to be inexact, what to select from the original and how to stress it in the translation.

When looking at a view a man instinctively selects and rejects. He does not have to be an artist to do this; his eye tells him what parts of the landscape are worth looking at. The sculptor, when looking at a human being, knows at once what needs emphasizing sculpturally. If he is a good sculptor he will emphasize, but with caution, the significant; if he is a bad sculptor he will emphasize, and without caution, the insignificant. The one develops the character of the object, the other produces a caricature of the object. The one is formative, the other deformative.

Admittedly the caricature has played its part in sculpture—Daumier worked the theme successfully enough in bronze—and even the grotesque has come to be canonized by the devotees of Gothic spout-heads, capitals, and misericords. But this sort of thing, to be sculpturally justified, has to be very well done indeed. It has to rely upon the principles of carving and not upon the laugh. It is as easy to get lost in the grotesque as it is to get lost in the sentimental, the naturalistic, the archaic. When carving surrenders to the grotesque there is little to keep it from the gross.

The sculptor who studies the created order with respect will think twice before he forces from it a twisted type. He will question beforehand the emphasis which he wants to give, subjecting it to the various lights of truth without which he must work in mental darkness. The grotesque in sculpture may be wrong for many reasons—it may offend against good taste, against charity, against religion, against the environment in which it is set—but the reason which most often puts it in the wrong is that it offends against the principle of proportion.

v

The last of the requirements to be mentioned in this preliminary and very general review is that of reasonably good execution. While craftsmanship is a long way from being the whole story, the lack of craftsmanship may spoil the story. Sculpture, as Sir Joshua Reynolds observed with weight, is a serious business. A man must have before him, when he sets out on the job, a definite purpose; he must further display some measure of ability in carrying it out. Execution is the only thing which he has got to show for the more important thing that has been going on inside his head.

It is one thing to hack out a rough object which

will do for a bird-bath in a garden; it is another to design and bring to its decent conclusion a sculptural composition. There are those who imagine that the rude, spontaneous flourish of the inexpert chisel can better indicate talent, and yield better results, than can thoughtful planning and hard work. Championship of the spontaneous, provided it leads the neophyte to a study of the craft, is to the good; the trouble is that it can lead to condoning the slapdash. While spontaneity may be part of the creative act, casualness can never be.

At the heart of all these sculptural principles lies the idea of creation. It is an analogy which never fails. (We shall meet it again when comparing the work of man's hands with the works of nature.) Just as God did not create in a mood of absent-mindedness, so neither can man. If man is to produce pieces of true sculpture, he must have his wits about him: there must be finish to his work, not enthusiasm only. A good hunk of stone is better than a bad bird-bath. Even a bad hunk of stone is better than a bad Venus.

"Sculpture," said Eric Gill, "is a matter of both workmanship and design."[14] Taken by itself neither technical dexterity nor imaginative conception can get very far. It is for the workmanship to prove the quality of the conception. This is why, having considered some

[14] *Op. cit.*, p. 41.

of the canons of workmanship, we can now begin to think of the conception. Where the inspiration has religion as its source and term, the activity which follows the inspiration will be a religious one. The sculptural expression which emerges from a mind informed by faith has now not only a new purpose to serve but also a deeper experience from which to draw. Added to the knowledge which comes by the senses there is the knowledge of truth and beauty which comes by faith. The wonder is that man can separate the ultimate mysteries of truth and beauty from those which are revealing themselves all round him, can appreciate the relative while forgetting about the absolute.

2. Less Remote

ALTHOUGH the approach to explicitly religious sculpture is by way of sculpture generally, the understanding of all true sculpture comes by way of the religious approach. That this is not just a partisan view, a propaganda actuation in the cause of religion, it will be the job of the present chapter to show. So far we have been judging sculpture in terms of the physical convex object which weighs this and measures that, which is made of a certain material and carved with certain tools. But this is only the patina of the subject, the surface texture. From now onwards we consider sculpture in terms of its spiritual content. Not yet as denominationally Christian and Catholic, but first as generically religious.

Strictly speaking, *all* true sculpture, and *only* true sculpture, is religious sculpture. Whatever there is that is good about a good piece of carving is good precisely because it reflects the truth and beauty of God. In the measure that it succeeds in this act of reflection it is a true and beautiful object; in the measure that it fails it is bad carving, false and ugly. Bad works of sculpture, however religious the subjects represented, are irreligious: they do not bear witness to the pattern of truth and beauty which is God himself. The degrees of goodness and badness in sculpture depend upon the approximation of the work to the absolute standard held out by the truth and beauty of God.

Where this doctrine is accepted and acted upon there follows a consistent, religious, integrated, and *strictly sculptural* tradition. Where it is neglected there is no tradition but only a series of reactions. The amorphous developments in our own age, for instance, are evidence of mental and spiritual confusion. Lacking primary values, sculptors cannot but apply secondary valuations. Where an activity which has for its realization a primary object is judged according to secondary standards there is bound to be confusion. The less interested you are in ultimate realities the more you fall back upon the interest provided by your own experience and your own desires. So of course your sculpture becomes egocentric, impulsive, esoteric.

In those ages of history when men recognize the same absolute standards there is not the same struggle in sculpture as can be seen today. In every age there will always be a straining towards the expression of an

47

ideal, but when the ideal is agreed upon the tension lies within a certain defined relationship. Where there is no clear relationship, where a new ideal is guessed at every year, where the standards applied give no absolute assurance, there cannot but be a sense of nervousness, conflict, arrogant empiricism in the expression. Man cannot help looking for truth and beauty, as he cannot help looking for happiness, but if he does not look in the right direction he will fling out right and left. The tension will become more marked as he goes on, and the execution will become more extravagant.

Originally the religious approach to sculpture was taken for granted. It was not as a specialized branch of aesthetics that the facts about God's absolute beauty were taught to the carvers of the Palaeolithic Age. The connection between the religious and the sculptural was assumed. This is not to claim that the first images fashioned by the hand of man were designed to depict God or to inspire reverence; it is to claim that the works of man's hands were seen as essentially related to a type which lay beyond both the material and the man carving it. Even if the earliest images are concerned more with magic than with worship—"[Primitive] man's entire activity," says Dr. Germain Bazin, "was aimed at skilfully intervening in the play of natural forces, in the hope of preserving a balance, attracting good and repelling evil powers"[1]—at least they show a common and innate subordination of the physical to the spiritual.

As the prehistorical stage in man's development gave place to the protohistorical, the development of sculpture was given new impetus by the discovery of new metals. The use of bronze, which was hammered and not cast, came in about 3500 B.C. It was in this era that the Elamite, Sumerian, and Aegean civilizations were flourishing. Since bronze could be had in greater quantity than the gold, silver, and copper which had been discovered centuries before, the advance which it occasioned was considerable. The tools used for carving bronze were still of polished stone, and so remained until iron-working techniques were evolved about 1400 B.C. in Asia Minor. Iron, still a rare metal in the Near East in the first half of the second millennium, reached the West much later. What we call the Iron Age lasted for two thousand years, reaching to the Christian era.

During all this time the theme of sculpture fluctuated a good deal, and it would be absurd to pretend that religion was always the predominant impulse. But this much can be said in confirmation of our thesis: first that the highest level of creative expression coincides with the primitive phase of the Stone Age, when man had little opportunity of cultivating materialistic ideas;

[1] *Concise History of Art,* p. 11.

49

and second that during the several thousands of years between the Magdalenian era and the rise of the Egyptian, Assyrian, Persian, Chaldean, and Syrian civilizations—a gap which showed a steady artistic decline—the outlook of mankind turned increasingly towards materialism. Only with the emergence of new ideas among the peoples of south-west Asia and the Nile did the old supernatural values reassert themselves.

Our contention can be further supported by the fact that most of the traditions of sculpture existing before the Christian era which went in for representational treatment ended up finally in adopting the symbolic and even the directly religious. Scenes of hunting, fishing, waging war, tended to bring in gods of hunting, fishing, war. The illustration of a hero's exploits, the desire to immortalize in stone or metal the memory of a king, the graphic decoration of a tomb: these things are forms of chief-worship, and for even the most elementary chief-worship there must be a certain deistic standard to which the chief is supposed to conform.

Nowhere was the apotheosis idea more developed, with its consequent effect upon sculpture, than among the Greeks and Romans. In the earlier stages of both civilizations the supernatural was the accepted background of life, and if the religious element is more evident where Greek than where Roman sculpture is concerned, it is because the attitude of Greece towards the supernatural was the more sincere.

Not so long ago it was thought necessary, if one hoped to get on in the world of sculpture, to carve in the manner of the Greeks. The *Laocoön* and the *Venus of Milo* were standard. The worst periods of the Greek tradition were held up for admiration for no other reason than that they were Greek. "We cannot," says Epstein, "go on eternally working like the Greeks; in order to do that it is necessary to think like the Greeks. We can learn what the Greeks had to teach, and adapt it to our own times."[2] If we think as the Greeks thought, philosophically and socially and religiously, then by all means let us carve as the Greeks carved; if we think as Christians, we must carve as Christians. It is because nineteenth-twentieth century thought has been neither Greek nor Christian that the returns to earlier styles have been so miscast. If there is one revival more inappropriate than the Classical Revival it is the Gothic.

The Romans had a particular gift for portraiture, and this, together with their feeling for civic grandeur, tended to overlay the religious quality of their inheritance. The link between the Roman and Greek traditions was Etruscan art,[3] which flourished between the

[2] *The Sculptor Speaks*, p. 77.
[3] Chiefly remarkable for works of clay and bronze, and for

seventh and fifth centuries B.C. If Rome had stuck to the Etruscan model, the Italian contribution to sculpture would probably have been greater than it was. The Etruscans went behind the Greek tradition, geographically as well as historically, reflecting much of Assyrian and Babylonian perception. Roman sculpture of the Republican period, leaving the Etruscan for the Greek, became increasingly naturalistic and impressive but also increasingly dull. On monuments and coins, in theatres and baths and arenas, the Greek sensibility was enviously aspired to by the newer race.[4] But what

---

designs made on imported earthenware. Belonging to central Italy, the Etruscans were too far away to be controlled by Greek conventions. Etruscan art has been called a "provincial extension" of Greek art.

[4] "This [the Greek aesthetic] carried all before it in the last years of the Republic, when the Roman aristocracy were fired with enthusiasm for conquered Greece and vied with one another for originals or copies of the masterpieces of Greek art. Caesar began the great transformation of Rome into the Imperial capital by enriching it with great monuments: a forum, a theatre, the Basilica Aemilia, the Basilica Julia, the Curia Julia. What is called 'Augustan' art emerged from a great Greco-Roman synthesis of political theory; for Augustus wanted to found a Roman classicism in both literature and art which would be worthy of its Hellenic model and which would become the typical culture of the Empire . . . the Antonine period was one of active building all over the Empire. Hadrian, thoroughly steeped in Greek culture, tried to

these prosperous Romans did not realize was that the Greek, for all its affinities to other styles, does not mix.

Another thing which these prosperous Romans did not realize was that a weakening of religious faith spells a weakening of religious art. Whatever the faith to be affected by humanism, humanistic carving comes out of it as a consequence. Debase the idea of absolute perfection and you debase the means of reflecting it. Styles and traditions of sculpture depend more upon the orientation of prevailing thought than upon any number of prevailing masters. The reason why this is not immediately evident is that the masters are almost always the products of their society. The society which worships God produces men who worship God in their work. A civilization usually gets the artists it deserves.

Allowing for differences of race and technical opportunity, it would be true to say that there is something in their sculptural expression which all religions hold in common. By the same token a common quality, or a common absence of quality, can be traced in the work of those who profess no religion. The carving of the South Sea islander may bear little resemblance to that of the sophisticated Greek, but if the gods are the same in each case there is bound to be an affinity somewhere.

---

perpetuate the images of the finest Hellenic works of architecture in his villa at Tivoli."—Bazin, *op. cit.*, p. 102.

Peoples whose gods are money or luxury or war will resemble one another in their carving. Their images will vastly differ from those of a people who worship God.

By placing empire before worship, the greatest potential influence in the world lost its chance. In forfeiting its soul, Rome forfeited also its claim to true sculpture. We have now come up to the Christian era and to a quite new inspiration.

ii

While the approach as here planned is not the historical so much as the psychological, spiritual, aesthetic and practical, a rough outline of the periods will be a help to the understanding of Christian sculpture. It is not the chronology that matters, but the sequence in the evolution of ideas. Without some grasp of the continuity, with its swing of action and reaction, the different schools of Christian carving are liable to be seen in isolation. The interesting thing about Christian carving is not the independence of the various traditions as they appear but their relationship.

It is always a matter of disappointment to reflect that the first wave of Christian enthusiasm was practically barren of sculptural expression. Reasons can be given for this. "Art does not flourish," writes Sir Leigh Ashton, "where its productions are likely to be destroyed. In Europe, through the chaotic centuries which followed the disintegration of the Western Roman Empire, material conditions were unfavourable to progress in the fine arts. In Europe the limited culture of the barbarian invaders was concerned mainly with decorative objects of personal adornment, jewellery and weapons. Elsewhere the Eastern Byzantine Empire evolved an independent style, while certain outposts, such as Alexandria, Ireland, and North Britain, established local schools which exercised a varying degree of general influence."[5]

But it was not solely because Christianity had to go underground during its infancy that there was little sculptural manifestation of the Church's spiritual vitality. Another, and perhaps more cogent, reason was that Christians had inherited from their Hebrew ancestors a certain suspicion of carved objects. If graven images had been a stumbling-block before, might they not be the same again? There seemed to be all the more danger now—now that God had revealed himself in a human body, and when Christ's mother and the saints were familiar to them as people, and when the martyrs' deaths were calling for a perpetuation of their memory—that the carving of statues would lead the newly converted back to the old temptations of false worship.

[5] *Style in Sculpture,* p. 9.

It must be remembered, moreover, that the world-civilization in which primitive Christianity found itself provided nothing in the way of a spiritual tradition in sculpture to which Christian carving could attach itself. If it was no good looking to Rome, it was no good looking to Athens either. Technically there was much to be learned, but religiously there was nothing to be developed. The Greeks, like the Romans after them, had too early turned away from their gods. There was nothing left of religion but metaphysics.

Lacking an existing line of spirituality which could be Christianized, the carvers of the first Christian centuries either borrowed from the classical tradition or else sharpened their chisels and waited.[6] As Merovingian influences began to make themselves felt in

[6] Historians seem to have stressed this dearth of early Christian carving too much. In van der Meer and Mohrmann's *Atlas of the Early Christian World* (Nelson, 1958) there are plates showing thirty-six examples of sculpture carved between the second and fifth centuries. Taking into consideration that such a catalogue is not meant to be exhaustive, and that the part of the world represented was just that part where every effort was made to stamp out every trace of Christian worship, the evidence is formidable. Furthermore it seems likely from the specimens which survive that carving went on during the early phases of the Byzantine movement. The reason why the specimens are so few is not because interest in sculpture abruptly ceased, but because the later exponents of the Byzantine style did their best to obliterate the work of their fathers.

Europe, awakening in the minds of men the desire to replace the lost culture with something new, an artistic expression came into being which was spiritual, Christian, untainted by the humanism of the classical decline. This was the art of Byzantium.

Byzantine art had a clear field and made the most of it. Since order had returned to Europe there was now no need to confine one's expression to the walls of tombs and secret meeting-places. There was a general demand for the decoration and furnishing of newly built, or newly adapted, Christian churches; there was material to be had; there was freedom of transport such as had not been known before; above all there was the need to direct the minds of the faithful, in an age when visual instruction was second only to oral, towards the eternal truths of Christianity.

After the voice of art had spoken in whispers for nearly five centuries, you would expect it to utter its message aloud in a strange accent. But though stiff and stilted in articulation, its speech was far from hesitant. As regards actual statuary, the Byzantine expression was never prolific. Perhaps there still lingered this inherited prejudice against the image in the round. Whatever they lacked in three-dimensional achievement, however, Byzantine artists made up for it in icons, ivory reliefs, and the new idiom of the mosaic.

In order to see Byzantine art in proper perspective,

we must see it as the outcome of forces other than artistic. Its whole outlook was revolutionary. Once Christians had decided to make use of the visual at all in their system of worship and instruction, they decided to apply the strictest sanctions. Imagery was to be a means towards worship, was to take its place as part of the Gospel apostolate, was to represent a complete negation of Greek and Roman humanism. Naturalism, the stress which had been given to physical beauty and temporal values, was to be attacked in line, form, import; supernaturalism was to be enshrined in its place. Since the Christian ethic stood for two principles, the one ascetic and the other mystical, the Christian expression in art must deny the earthly and point unequivocally to the heavenly. No approach could be more direct and logical than the Byzantine.

Now that the figurative was taking the place of the representational, the symbol and not the model became the main thing. Art was getting back to its original idea. But where men before had sought by magic to bring God down from heaven into the works of their hands, they now sought to raise their minds in prayer to God through the instrumentality of their works. Art in the Byzantine conception became a language between the individual soul and God, between the layman and the theologian, between the Church and the rest of the world. Art was thought of as conveying the Word, the *logos,* the word "which must not return to

God void" and which had been made flesh for man's salvation.

All this led in practice to certain clearly defined techniques as regards composition and the portrayal of the human figure. Since the whole thing relied on the immediate understanding of the symbol, everything had to be discarded which might get in the way of the symbol's impact. Bazin (whose favourite style is not the Byzantine) gives the following fair account: "Some compositions were reduced to a few forms linked together like words in a statement, reminding us of hieroglyphs. Images were now unreally suspended as though in flight, against an abstract gold background; the line of the horizon disappeared, together with the earth itself. Events no longer took place on the earth or in the sky but in an ideal universe. The figures in the composition no longer had the relative sizes that would be theirs in concrete reality, but their size was now determined by the idea behind them: as in the early Egyptian and Mesopotamian arts, the principal person in the composition towered over all the rest, who were grouped like dwarfs at his feet. The composition of landscape was treated with the same severity, a mountain becoming a mere mound of sand, or a building no larger than a footstool. A purely moral hierarchy replaced the material order of things."[7]

The Byzantine formula appealed, as may be imag-

[7] *Op. cit.*, pp. 119, 120.

Approach to Christian Sculpture

ined, far more to the East than to the West. Borrowing more from the Eastern tradition of a thousand years before than from classical Greece and Rome, the Byzantine influence spread through the countries which came to be identified with the Orthodox Church more rapidly, and as it turned out more lastingly, than it spread in the West.[8] It was not that Western Europeans could not understand symbolism when they saw it; it was simply that they were everywhere surrounded, as Western Asians were not surrounded, by relics of the classical tradition. Culture to the West European meant classical culture. The art which developed in Christian Europe had more to unlearn.

In Northern Europe the situation was different. Here there was nothing to unlearn. Here the symbolical and mystical had it all its own way. Though more ornamental than the Byzantine which was taking root east of Constantinople (Byzantium), Celtic and Anglo-Saxon art resisted the elaborations which their Christian brethren were going in for further south. Another difference was this: the Northerners felt no inhibitions about carving. Thus while the feeling for volume was on the decline in Eastern Christendom—partly as a deliberate reaction against the Greeks, and partly on

[8] Where Byzantine art is called "Greek," the connection is with the Greek Church, and not with the Greek culture, to which it was on all counts opposed.

60

account of the preoccupation with line and the specialized technique of mosaic—it was by no means dead in the rest of the Christian world.

This brings us to the eighth and ninth centuries when, in the West, Byzantium's day was almost over. Like other traditions before and since, the Byzantine carried its theories too far. It made a cult of flatness; it demanded mathematical symmetry; it refused to suggest movement. In its revolt against naturalism it revolted not only against the suggestion of perspective—allowing now only full front-face or full profile to representations of the head—but against any kind of sculptured rendering of the human form. The movement had become so spiritualized that it was in danger of abandoning the Incarnation. And this is where the Church stepped in.

Influenced by the Muslim, now entrenched in the Mediterranean theatre of Christendom, a Byzantine faction began preaching the sinfulness of statuary. The movement might have spread, and iconoclasm triumphed, had not the Church in both East and West repudiated the idea. At Byzantium itself a reaction against oriental aesthetics and theologies set in. So that the ninth century saw a Macedonian revival in eastern Europe which was matched during the tenth century by the Carolingian renaissance in the West. The compromise traditions which resulted were not of a quality to last, and only in the eleventh century did an art come into being which was to fulfil the requirements alike of aesthetics and theology. In the Romanesque conception, indeed, theology and aesthetics were one. Such a union had not been achieved before, and it has been achieved since only for the briefest periods and in particular regions.

iii

If a good deal of space has been devoted to the Byzantine tradition, which in any case was not sculptural but linear, the reason is twofold. First, as the earliest artistic expression of Christianity the Byzantine style provides norms to be referred to in the consideration of later periods. In every movement, whether ideological, religious, or artistic, it is the initial manifestation that must be looked at: subsequent developments can to a large extent be judged by their approximation to the original idea. Though the Byzantine theory ran away with itself in the end, it established sound principles when it was first proclaimed. It is to these principles, partly artistic and partly religious, that we shall be returning in our review of later schools. The second reason for giving Byzantium so prominent a place is that the Romanesque, though at two removes,[9] derived very largely from it.

[9] Namely the Macedonian Revival and the Carolingian school.

The Romanesque approach to art in general (and for our purpose here to sculpture) was evolved not in Italy but in France. Italian Romanesque dates from nearly two centuries later, roughly 1250 A.D.[10] Eleventh century France gave more to art than any other country in any other period. The Italian Renaissance of the fifteenth century may have made a greater display, but the French Romanesque made a greater impression. The effect of Romanesque can be judged by the style which followed it: where Renaissance art led on to Baroque, Rococo, and Romanticism, the Romanesque tradition led on to Gothic at its purest.

Romanesque carving was ushered in not by painting, as in the case of some schools of sculpture, but by architecture. This in itself was a good sign: it made for discipline, balance, and three-dimensional design. Where Byzantine churches had allowed mosaics, icons and mural drawings to fill spaces anywhere which were not filled already, the Romanesque principle of architecture demanded the strictest order in church decoration: everything was planned to lead up to various key points in the building. There was nothing haphazard, either in composition or in detail, about the Romanesque interpretation. Where the Byzantine de-

[10] The name Romanesque has nothing to do with Rome; it was applied centuries later on account of the romance language which was the dialect in the part of France where "Romanesque" architecture was first tried.

signers had stressed the most significant element of their compositions by eliminating every detail which might distract from it, the designers of the new school achieved the same result by carving in depth and relating the detail to the central interest. Sculpture, at last, came into its own.

So it is that we can find in Romanesque all the best features both of the Byzantine which went before and the Gothic which came after—with none of the extravagances which spoiled either of them. It combined the old feeling for symbolism, harmony, restraint, and spirituality with a new energy and sensitivity. The symbolism now was as dynamic as the truths symbolized. Inheriting from iconography and the mosaics a sense of unemotional mysticism, the carvings of the Romanesque school kept faithfully to the original purpose, which was to teach dogma and raise the soul to God in worship. The ultimate mysteries are the stuff of Romanesque sculpture, and if we think of it only as the decorative use of a formula, as the stylized transcription of things seen quite differently in nature, as a mannered and highly sophisticated idiom it means that we have missed its whole significance.

Like every other style the Romanesque evolved its own conventions, which it applied with greater strictness than most, but it did not allow its conventions to cramp its spontaneity. Nothing, not even the Gothic, could have been more creative and dynamic. The Romanesque is the only style of which it may be said that it was both traditional and progressive, doctrinal as well as free. It exactly reflected, as it has been our argument that every age of sculpture must reflect, the age. The formulation of dogma and the development of contemplation: these characteristics of the early Middle Ages reveal themselves in all the most typical examples of Romanesque carving. Fortunately it was not for some five centuries to come that sentiment and virtuosity were to take the place of the transcendental.

The carved Christ of the eleventh and twelfth century is above all the King, the Crowned Saviour, the Head of the Mystical Body. The Mother of God is not so much the tender woman as the august queen. If we look here for human loveliness we are disappointed, but we find instead a dignity and power which are far more moving. There is mystery in the Romanesque Mother of God which is lacking in the Madonna of even the best Gothic period. It is significant that we refer naturally to the Gothic "Madonna," or the Renaissance or the Baroque "Madonna," the implication being that of personal relationship and intimacy: in speaking about Romanesque carving we are more likely to refer to the "Mother of God"—the *Theotokos* legacy handed down from the Byzantines.

We who belong to a quite different way of thinking,

even as Christians, have a quite different perception. Our eternal values, when we sit down to think of them, may be exactly the same as those professed by Catholics of the twelfth century; but we have to sit down to think of them. To the man of the twelfth century the true perspectives were habitual—or he could not have carved as he did or else could not have understood what he carved. The vision which expressed itself in the carved tympanum over the west door at Vezelay, an apocalyptic composition which typifies Romanesque thought and technique, has been lost for good. Without the same sense of awe we of our own age see Christ, his Mother, the saints, the Church and the Church's doctrines in different perspective.

When the vision of light and truth fades, the criteria of artistic achievement drop to a different level. "It is a lovely statue of our Lady: she smiles so sweetly." "Why do you make Saint Joseph look so stern? I am sure he was really such a nice, understanding person." "These modern sculptors have forgotten what babies look like, and that is why they do the Infant Jesus all wrong." But religious carving is meant to be a plea for light and truth, not for charm. No period states this more clearly than the Romanesque. In the last analysis religious carving stands or falls by whether or not it is the formulated recognition of the primacy of God in his created world.

What all Christians learn through the senses and through grace, the Christian sculptor tries to express through the medium of his craft. The outward work is pointing to the immanence of God, to the one supremely important reality. Everything else relates to this, the presence of God on earth and in heaven. Wherever the theme is obscured by decoration, however sculpturally conceived the decoration may be, there is fault. This is not to say that Romanesque carving fell into the trap of confusing the subject with the content—the men of that period knew better than to claim as religious sculpture only the examples which depicted religious scenes—but rather to say that the value of sculptural decoration was judged in relation to the essential thing which it decorated. The essential thing was religion.

All too often, and inevitably, Romanesque art departed from the old Byzantine ideal of simplification. But what mattered to the newer school much more than abstraction was the substantial form which abstraction tended to neglect. Simplifying the treatment is no good if what is expressed by the treatment is seen as stylized and not as purified. Though Romanesque designs tended to become complicated, the essential content continued to find expression with extreme directness and simplicity. For all its richness, Romanesque carving was saved from flamboyance by the intrinsic purity of its inspiration. The Gothic, centuries later, was to degenerate into ornamentation; the Romanesque kept decoration in its place.[11]

To close this section on Romanesque carving a passage from M. Bazin may be quoted. According to him "Romanesque [art] had no very deep religious bearing," so he would not agree with half of what has been said above, but he must be heard nevertheless. "It is a surge of forms elbowing each other, merging one into the other on arch mouldings, pilasters, tympana, spandrels and capitals. Everything from the very beginnings of mankind came together to enrich this marvellous language in stone: pagan myths and Christian scenes, fragments of antiquity, barbarous ornament, Byzantine, Sassanian, Assyrian and even Sumerian forms, for the old animal symbolism of the cylinder-seals of Sumeria and Elam found its final transformation here. Western man, as he started creating once again after six centuries, began by remembering; but he used all the forms that he remembered from the depths of the past as though they were words, creating a new language with them which he spoke with a wonderful oratorical ease."[12]

[11] In illustration of twelfth-century carving where ornament plays the supporting role there are the elaborate tympana at Charlieu and at Neuilly-en-Donjon. The capitals at Issoire, belonging to the same century, are instances of the same thing.

[12] *Op. cit.*, p. 154.

If in the foregoing pages we have tried to show that the Romanesque style, borrowing from the Church itself, showed marks of unity, holiness, and apostolicity, then the above quotation would indicate that the note of catholicity was not wanting either.

iv

It would be a mistake to think of the Gothic style as suddenly bursting upon Western Europe and sweeping all before it. Equally it would be a mistake to think of the Romanesque as petering out because it had stuck too closely to the text-book. Rather it was a case of the text-book taking on new articles, being rewritten in the idiom of the time, and coming out under a new title. It was not the Byzantine story over again. Western Byzantine art had, as we have seen, come to grief partly because it had worked its theory to death and partly because it had played with the errors of Islam and Greece. The Romanesque tradition never came to grief at all, but merely merged quite naturally into the Gothic. As always, the art was following the thought: with the thirteenth century the thought of western Christendom was becoming warmer.

That the transition was not as abrupt as some would like to make it can be seen in the carvings at Chartres and Notre Dame. Both are early thirteenth century, both would bear the label Gothic, but it would be absurd to say that the new sculpture had discarded the principles of the old. Architecturally the Gothic designers may have invented a new style, but sculpturally they were merely adapting and humanizing the old.

But even granted that the Gothic is only the Romanesque grown to maturity, that it is the same twelfth-century theological figure made human with devotion, there is much about the Gothic carver that marked the innovator. Symbols of the human race became representations of human beings, and the idea tended to give place to the person. Just as the theology of the Sacred Humanity was directing the contemplative life of the Church along channels that had been in danger of either drying up or flowing eastwards, so in the Church's sculptural expression a certain anthropomorphism was beginning to replace the ideomorphism which still showed Eastern ancestry.

But humanizing influences are tricky things to control. The Gothic interpretation spread fast, and at first happily, but it followed the course of those other movements in art that have made too many concessions to popular demand. If classical sculpture went through its phases until it ended up in frank naturalism, ecclesiastical sculpture cannot be blamed for going the same way. The wonder is that the Gothic style lasted so long, spread so far, and has been so consistently revived. Certainly it is significant that the Eternal City would have none of it. Indeed Italy as a whole—standing out in this against not only France, which was the birthplace of the Gothic, but also against England, Germany, Spain, and the Low Countries—remained to the end suspicious of what it regarded as too fancy for serious consideration. To Italy the Gothic continued to be, for rather more than two centuries, a novelty—a dangerously dominating novelty. Italy's turn was to come with the Renaissance.

While Gothic carving can be classified almost indefinitely, according to the degree of elaboration it went in for, according to the architectural mood which it served, according to the different countries where it flourished and the local schools which interpreted it, it answers readily enough to the simple and unprofessional classification which divides into liturgical sculpture and devotional sculpture. The liturgical tended to be solemn, the devotional to be light. In the end of course it was the devotional that won. People prefer the light.

It is a curious fact that while in England the Gothic style of carving was almost always solemn, in Germany it was almost always spirited. You would have thought it would be the other way round. As regards England it was an advantage because when the English lose their sense of solemnity in sculpture they are apt to produce *Peter Pan* in Kensington Gardens, or, at worst, gnomes. We do better to risk being pompous, and stick to gravity. In contrast there is the lively Gothic of Bavaria and the Rhine. The final phase of Germany's Gothic career (late fifteenth century) with its triptychs, altar-pieces, angels, crowns, broken folds and mannered poses is just as charming as the Baroque and scarcely less theatrical.

But in spite of variations in rendering, the factor which remained common and constant in Gothic carving was that of faith. The Gothic expressed the religious aspiration of the whole society. While it taught by allegory and scriptural illustration, it did not have to be as didactic as the earlier schools. The Byzantine and the Romanesque were determined to teach, and teach they did. If the Byzantine and Romanesque are imposing, it is to some extent because they imposed. There the Church and the artist were dictating; the layman was taking it in. But here, in the case of the Gothic, the layman was at one with the effort of the Church and the artist. The style came as much from below as from above. Gothic is generally liked because it is in the strict sense popular. If Gothic is also, like the Byzantine and Romanesque, imposing, this is because it had almost the whole weight of Europe behind it.

The nobility of the original conception, however, did not last. By the end of the fourteenth century there were all the signs of decadence. The humanity which had been awakened a hundred and fifty years before was degenerating into sentimentality, prettiness, refinement. Gothic was becoming *embourgeoisé.* "Wealth became more generally distributed, and, through trade, fortunes were rapidly made," writes Leigh Ashton, accounting for the Gothic decline. "By asserting their burgher-rights, the merchants and townsmen obtained a greater share of political power. These provided a new market for works of art which themselves reflect something of the shrewdness, vigour, and hardheadedness that had won this class its financial and political position. A taste for the practical and natural ousts the fourteenth-century predilection for elegance and preciosity. As the century moves forward, this naturalistic bias is increasingly pronounced, though as it closes the new style has been enriched by exuberant adjuncts in treatment in detail, particularly drapery."[13]

The same author further points out how the Guilds at this period exercised a stranglehold on artistic output, and how the demand for mass-produced carving led inevitably to aesthetic stagnation. Both the curve of Gothic achievement and the combination of forces

[13] *Op. cit.,* p. 27.

which bore upon it can be seen as exactly reflecting the experience of the Greeks.

The beginning of the fifteenth century saw the stirring of a new mood. Already the craftsmen of the Renaissance, infiltrating northwards by way of Nüremburg, Augsburg, and the prosperous cities along the trade-route from the south, were attacking the strongholds of the Gothic. If carvers of the Gothic had turned their hands to naturalistic treatment, here were these cunning Italians who could do it far better.

But before considering the sculpture of the Renaissance we must attempt a summing up of the contribution made by the carvers of the Gothic. In the first place they brought back a feeling for the round. Where the Romanesque tradition in stone is remarkable chiefly for its reliefs, the Gothic is seen to be equally at home with the complete figure. In the second place Gothic carvers gave themselves greater sculptural liberty than had been known in the Church before their time. Where the Romanesque was more single-minded, the Gothic was less doctrinaire. In the third place Gothic carvers were uninhibited in their religious expression.

This combination of roundness, sculptural liberty, and religious enthusiasm resulted in a clearly recognizable type. The Gothic figure is not easily mistaken. It is of all types the most generally accepted as "re-

ligious." Our argument would be that the carvings
are religious not only because the faces mostly wear
a pious expression but because the work was performed in a religious spirit. If Gothic figures suggest
the idea of religion it is because to the people of the
Gothic centuries sculpture and personal religion were
related in a way which had never quite been realized
before and which has certainly never been repeated
since.

The claim is not that Gothic carvers were all men
of piety; the claim is that the men who quarried the
stone, the men who did the transporting and putting in
position, the men who looked at the finished work and
paid for it, the men who thought about it and criti-
cized it and forgot about it were all at one with the
man who conceived and executed the work in affirm-
ing the same supernatural faith. When the workmen
and the people for whom they work are in agreement
about God, who is absolute beauty, the work itself will
reflect the direction of the thought.

v

Renaissance carving, for all its connection with the
new learning, did not start off on intellectual lines; it
started off merely on independent lines. The first demand was for perfect execution in a particular *genre*;
culture came later. So far as religion was concerned the

sculptor of the Renaissance was no longer expected, as sculptors of an earlier tradition had been expected, to teach. It was now every man for himself, and if he carved religiously, so much the better. For Gothic, Romanesque, Byzantine art, the faith was the firmament; for Renaissance art it was only the church-space. Religion and a study of the classics provided subjects to be illustrated; the actual inspiration was supposed to come from inside the artist himself.

The result was only to be expected: eclecticism, secularization, the glorification of the individual. "Men can do all things if they will," cried Alberti, the apostle of the new art, and men found themselves willing to do all things at once. Where hitherto the craftsman had worked as an anonymous member of the community— whether the town, guild, province or country—he now assumed a name and could sign it on the works of his hands for future generations to read. If his religious principles were no longer determined by the race to which he belonged, neither were the principles of his carving. Renaissance sculpture was the first in history which did not represent a collective way of thinking, a collective sculptural interpretation. The idea of a social group producing things of a kind was lost, and instead it became a question of personal achievement. Ghiberti, Donatello, Michelangelo, Riccio, Verrocchio, Bramante: great masters with great followings, but each one essentially unique, single, alone.

"The Renaissance, the New Poverty, marks the turning point for us," says Eric Gill, "and what happened then was this: man became critic where formerly he had been creator. Intrinsic values gave place to extrinsic, absolute to relative. Art which formerly conformed to absolute standards of knowledge and service was replaced by work which was valuable primarily as interpretation. The artist became the interpreter and his work the mirror of the world. The painter no longer made things which were themselves an integral part of nature. He made essays in the criticism of nature—pro or con. The great initiators of this new adventure soon gave place to the host of mere purveyors of the loveable—persons who make their livings by supplying representations of what they and their customers like."[14]

It is a mistake to think of Renaissance sculpture as a style: it is any number of individual people's styles which happen to agree on certain points. It is not a tradition so much as an absence of tradition. Tradition depends on corporate experience, but there was no corporate experience behind Renaissance sculpture: there was only contemporary experience. Even the Baroque which came later was, in spite of its anomalies, a style which emerged from a common, if superficial, experience.

If Renaissance carvings have a character of their

[14] *Sculpture*, pp. 14, 15.

own—the Muses and Virtues standing always in a high wind, athletic-looking angels with muscular arms and firm sturdy legs, prophets and bishops and politicians with the forefinger on an open book—it is the character of the non-essential, of the polished performance, of the terrestrial. The Renaissance manner of carving represented the experience of a few great sculptors, and it was the expression of their genuine feeling that was imitated and debased until a substitute was produced which passed for tradition.

Of Michelangelo's effect upon the sculpture of his age, Sir Jacob Epstein says that "his influence was so overpowering as to be fatal to his contemporaries and their followers. A genius such as Michelangelo is disastrous to the art of his country for many generations. Michelangelo expressed movement and violent action but with calm and serenity. His ideal was potential power and movement, which his followers misunderstood and translated into restlessness and over-muscled gesture."[15]

Nevertheless in making the statue more important than the painting, the sculptors of the Renaissance did a service to the art of carving. "No doubt sculpture owed its prominence," writes M. Bazin, "to the fact that it was an essentially physical art in a period whose main aim was to give their due to the beauty and

[15] *Op. cit.*, pp. 123, 124.

strength of the human body."[16] Once realism had been made a primary objective, moreover, it was felt that real dimensions were necessary. The false perspectives which are vital to the picture and to the relief were passed over in favour of the real perspectives obtained by placing carved figures in space. But it did not take long for Renaissance painting to catch up on Renaissance sculpture: painters were soon found who could give satisfaction with an appearance of reality which was so lifelike as to be almost magical.

The change of direction in sculpture from religious to secular did not come about either suddenly or as part of a policy. Ghiberti, for example, who was one of the first great names of the movement, went on with much that he had learned from the Gothic. While he and Donatello made continued use of the religious theme in the South, the Northern Renaissance was ushered in on the strictly religious work of Adam Krafft, Adolf Daucher, and Tilman Riemenschneider. But the change was bound to come, and in proportion as the Renaissance world concentrated increasingly on profane studies the interest in sacred sculpture waned. With the advance of this sophisticated era, carving became more complicated and individualistic in treatment, and in content more intellectual and rationalistic. It was the heyday of humanism after all.

[16] *Op. cit.,* p. 232.

By the second half of the century (the fifteenth) all idea of symbolical representation had gone. Donatello, now the leading exponent, was drawing upon Imperial Rome rather than upon Christian inspiration. Though he was imitated all over Italy, there was nobody who could compete with him for the dignity, intensity, sensitivity of his bronzes. Working in relief as well as in the round, Donatello displayed a versatility which must have been bewildering even to the quickly changing manners of the time. But always it was in the direction of naturalism, and always his disciples and rivals went the same way. Verrocchio, outliving the master by twenty-two years, tried it in bronze and perhaps came nearest to Donatello in feeling. Rosselino tried it in marble, and very nearly caught the master's grace. The names of Donatello and Michelangelo are linked together not because the two men worked in the the same way or because they worked within a half century of one another. They are linked because each in his own way was a creative genius, and it would have been impossible for such creative genius to have declared itself at any earlier period than the Renaissance. The Renaissance established once and for all, for better or for worse, the position of the artist in society. And Donatello and Michelangelo stood, in the minds of men, for the artist.

That any workman should so stand, and remain standing to this day, is deplored by Eric Gill. "The period of decay which the Renaissance ushered in began about four hundred and fifty years ago," booms this great man; "it is now past repair. We are in a sinking ship and each man must save himself. There is no question even of 'women and children first' for in this matter all are equal and no man can save another's soul."[17] But in the cycle of history and the order of God's grace nothing is as final as that. The different voices of the Renaissance are only echoes of the different voices raised at the building of Babel's tower. But other generations are born, and the art of building is learned anew. The different phases of Renaissance evolution are only duplications of what we have noted in earlier movements. It is possible that such a social order may arise in which the artist works as one of a tradition, a school, a tribe, and not simply as a would-be expert on his own. It is possible that a social order may arise which is in the full sense a community: a body of human beings who believe in the same things and who corporately seek to see them realized. It will not be Communism that will produce such a social order; it will, if it is given its chance, be Christianity.

vi

Baroque art, particularly religious Baroque art, is often hailed as a reaction against the ponderous aesthetic of the Renaissance. It may have amounted to

[17] *Op. cit.*, p. 17.

this in the long run, but its first expression was by no means a counter-revolution. Nor did it come suddenly —with the lightness and swiftness of flight suggested by its angels. Far from being a Christian crusade, it began as yet another manifestation of rationalism; far from being quick on the heels of Renaissance art, it developed out of a style called Mannerism which was briefly but significantly transitional.

Towards the close of the sixteenth century the spirit of empiricism and the tendency to question everything about existence, present and future, was manifested in sculpture by a certain cold intellectualism which was reminiscent once again of classical Greece. But no art can subsist indefinitely on a diet of philosophy and brain-searching, and the cautious sculpture which resulted from such a diet was due for a change.

Now that the new learning of the Renaissance was turning out to be only a very old learning in disguise, a division came about in sculpture which separated those who wanted to follow the classical way of formalism and those who wanted to experiment with something less stereotyped. So that out of the Renaissance creed which rested on the representation of human life as seen by reason came two quite different schools, Neo-Classicism[18] and what has been known as Mannerism.

[18] The label of Neo-Classicism is usually attached to an art which appeared somewhat later and in reaction against the

Where the two schools agreed was in the interpretation which they gave to man's existence on earth: for both it was a pageant.

The story of Neo-Classicism, since it has no bearing on Christian sculpture, need not detain us. It followed the usual sequences and continued into the present century. Classicism will probably be revived at intervals for as long as carving is practised. The story of Mannerism, however, calls for some slight attention here: it not only served as an overture to Baroque but was also the medium through which religion came back to sculpture.

Mannerism, though it numbered some big names in its following, is not one of the styles of which sculpture may be proud. It was a compromise between the legacy of Michelangelo and Hellenistic formalism. Coming out of an environment as disillusioned, and what we would now call "existentialist," as our own, it was sculpture's late sixteenth-century bid for attention. It was exhibitionist, unsure of itself, nervous. Bazin refers to "that exacerbation of style known as Mannerism." Italy was its home, and the only school to hold out against it was the Venetian. Its exponents in the field of sculpture were Bandini, Giovanni Bologna (a

---

Rococo. But since the earlier movement was working in the same direction as the later, the naming can be advanced so that it covers both.

83

Frenchman, surprisingly), Vittoria, and the metal-worker Benvenuto Cellini. In the field of painting there were many more, but we are not concerned with painting.

Leigh Ashton describes the movement as follows: "Technical virtuosity plays an ever more prominent part in the works of the sculptors who, in emulation of their great predecessor [Michelangelo], at first modified and then abandoned the canon of classical form. The system of anatomical distortion to which they had recourse, and the tendency to represent the body twisted like a corkscrew above the hips . . . are hall-marks of the movement known as Mannerism."[19] The movement is referred to as a crisis in the history of sculpture, but this is surely to take it too seriously. It was not so much a crisis as a neurosis. It was a tension working towards an eventual equilibrium.

One of the factors which kept Mannerism in being longer than it deserved was aristocratic patronage. Favoured first at the court of the Medici in Florence, the fashion spread to Fontainebleau, where it became the royal hobby. Another thing which prolonged the life of Mannerism, and one more closely connected with our subject, was the backing given to it by the Church. The Church, realizing that the effects both of the Renaissance and of Protestantism were likely to

[19] *Op. cit.*, p. 46.

continue, was launching its Counter-Reformation while at the same time trying to Christianize the humanism nearer home. Rome saw in Mannerism a possible vehicle for the combating of error and the propagation of the old faith. It was a return to the idea of Byzantium, which had proposed a visual presentation of religious truth. Mannerism might not be the most suitable style to choose for this, but the only alternative was Neo-Classicism, which was worse.

Mannerism accordingly, having no particular character of its own beyond the aptitude for originality, took on an explicitly religious turn. Nowhere was Christian Mannerism shown to better advantage than in Spain. Working mostly in stone, Alonso Berruguete popularized with his racked frames and anguished faces the new religious style of Latin Christendom. He was followed by Juan de Juni, Guido Mazzoni, Niccolo dell'Arca, and Pompeo Leoni, who, though not themselves Spanish, like Berruguete, carved in the same passionate idiom. Religious Mannerism had its adherents also in Germany, Protestant and Catholic alike, where the great names of Matthias Grünewald and Lucas Cranach are connected with it.

So as Mannerism gradually merged into Baroque, the Church merged with it. In fact the Baroque, its aesthetic more clearly defined and its technique more uniform than anything since the Gothic, proved in many ways a more promising movement for the Church to sponsor than Mannerism had been. There were drawbacks here too—for the new style was worldly, was of the theatre, was a little too sumptuous for Christian humility and a little too ebullient for Christian modesty, was hardly spiritual at all and by some might be thought even pagan—but at least it was beginning in Rome itself and so presumably could be controlled. In any case Mannerism had served its turn, and here on the move was something specifically Catholic, highly cultured, and full of fun.

vii

But though the Church was as ready to serve the cause of Baroque as Baroque was ready to serve the cause of the Church, the new style was far from being exclusively ecclesiastical. Indeed in its later developments it became, as we shall see, increasingly secular. Nor was its purpose to be full of fun. Gay as it was in expression, Baroque took itself very seriously. It even took its religion very seriously, though few outside the movement would have been willing to believe this.

Baroque sculpture was led and perfectly typified by Bernini, whose life and work extended over almost the whole of the seventeenth century.[20] Though the style

[20] Giovanni Lorenzo Bernini was born in 1598 and died in 1680.

had its origins in late Renaissance treatment, and particularly Michelangelesque treatment, it represented a complete change of feeling. The whole tempo was lighter and quicker. Gone were the firm thighs, strong wrists, brooding expressions, and in their place came rounded limbs and cheerful looks. The sculptors of the new Italian school were not out to record the deeper emotions—all that was for the Spanish, and later for the Romantics—so much as warmth and visual satisfaction. If a dramatic impression could be created, and if possible a religious dramatic impression, no more was asked.

Though the impression might be one of religion, the subject-matter and the setting being religious, there was little enough of religion in its content. Baroque carving was interested in the religious subject but not at all in the religious psyche. The Baroque felt no call to give impulse to eschatology, metaphysics, dogma or the liturgy; Christian glow, rather than Christian theology, was the objective. What references there were to death and an after-life were more for stage effect than for meditation.[21]

When the Baroque—taking with it its fluted gold

[21] Though a skeleton is introduced into two of Bernini's sculptural compositions, the tomb of Urban VIII and the tomb of Alexander VII, it is more as a stage prop than as anything else. Symbolism as such had no great interest for Bernini.

rays, elegant halos, bulging and bursting clouds—spread north to Germany, Austria, and Switzerland, it came into the prepared environment of late religious Mannerism. Here in these countries it glittered even more than before, radiating from every altar and shrine a light religious fervour all its own. In the wealth of lavish display, vivid representation, and energetic movement, the function of sculpture was reduced; carving was thought of only in relation to the decorative scheme. There were, it is true, in this early eighteenth-century period of Germanic Baroque, some good second- and third-rate sculptors with a nice butterfly touch, the best of whom were Georg Donner and Egid Quirin Asam, but for the most part the sculptor was not given a chance of appearing in his own right.

England would have none of it; to the English the Baroque smelled of incense and Rome and shifty-looking priests. But in Spain, meanwhile, the Baroque was being translated into the temperamental idiom of the race. The factors which kept Spanish Baroque under control, preventing it from going in the way of the French interpretation which will be examined below, were first the nature of Spanish architecture and second the nature of Spanish spirituality. The Romanesque building can defy the effect of an alien decoration, can even assimilate it and be enriched by it. Most of

the churches in Spain were either Romanesque or
strong early Gothic.[22] For such as showed Moorish influence, the more Baroque decoration the better.

Mention has been made of Mannerist work done in
Spain by two well-known sculptors, Berruguete and de
Juni. These were followed as more professedly
Baroque by Hernandez and Montañez, who represent
perhaps the finest achievement of the style in any
country. Certainly theirs is the most deeply religious
of any Baroque expression. No butterflies here, or
playful charm; this is the stern stuff of a truly, even of
a desperately, religious feeling. While the next generation of Spanish sculptors, represented by Pedro de
Mena and Alonso Cano, somewhat toned down the ex-
pressionism of their forerunners, the adamantly religious character of Spanish carving was continued.
And as such it has continued to this day. The Rococo
never touched the tradition, and if in our own time
Spaniards want to experiment in the Abstract manner,
they come away to other countries.

But now we turn to France, the country whose claim
to the development of Baroque must be equal to that
of Italy. With an eye for the histrionic, Louis XIV, liv-

[22] Compare the French Baroque of Rouen, for example, with
the Spanish Baroque of Compostela. In the one the decoration
kills the architecture, in the other the decoration is subordin-
ated by the architecture.

ing symbol of man's aristocratic superiority over lesser creatures, saw in the Baroque much what the Church had seen in Mannerism. It was a medium, and with its help the monarch turned the spotlight upon himself and upon his elegant, mundane, polite and dilettante court. The light was left on and the charade never stopped, and with each new season the masks grew more extravagant and there was ever more need for grease-paint. If elsewhere the Baroque was still the avowed religious style, in France it was frankly profane. The virtuosity remained but the spirit had changed. By the eighteenth century, Versailles, so far as sculpture and sculptural decoration went, had ousted Rome, and the Baroque had become Rococo.

Rococo, flourishing in the reigns of Louis XV and Louis XVI, was confined almost exclusively to France, where it was in the lead until the Revolution. Rivalry from Neo-Classicism, again Italian in origin, produced in Rococo a certain sobering effect but did not alter its purpose, which was to entertain. Suited to its pagan environment on the French Olympus, the new and now entirely secular Baroque lacked just that quality of astringency without which no style can expect to last. Sculpture, certainly, is not meant for spectacular fantasy; sculpture needs discipline as well as depths. So wanting was it at the end, even in the dramatic character which had impelled the style from which it derived, that the next artistic movement to declare itself in Europe, namely Romanticism, looked more to Neo-Classicism than to Rococo. The glow that had animated Italian, German, Austrian, Swiss, and Spanish Baroque was gone, and only the glitter was left.

viii

Apart from the Gothic Revival, the various schools that have come into being during the past hundred and fifty years bear only an accidental relation to Christian sculpture. It would be impossible within the scope of this book to go into the spiritual implications of the interest that has been shown in Mexican, African, Indian, and Chinese carving. Such interest is not on quite the same level as interests expressing themselves in Neo-Classicism and the Gothic Revival. Interest both in primitive tribes and in developed oriental civilizations is never likely to be very general, whereas interest in the Greek and the Gothic will always be with us: in the Greek partly for literary reasons, in the Gothic partly for sentimental reasons.

While taking no part, either way, in the nineteenth-century classical revivals, the Church took an eager part in the Gothic Revival. For the Church the last official style had been the Baroque, and having played horse to Baroque's Lady Godiva with increasing uneasiness for the best part of two hundred years, it was with some relief that the authorities could look this new movement squarely in the eye. It was respectable, it was something that the Church had known before and did not have to learn up afresh, it had endless material to refer to and endless possibilities to develop. The only thing against it was that it made for dullness when one had to do everything all over again, and especially when the spirit that had produced the original Gothic was only too signally lacking.

For this very reason—namely that it was not *of* the people but *for* the people—the sculpture of the Gothic Revival is without fire, sunlight, poetry, music, or anything much else. The figures look as though they had been carved from photographs late at night by sick men. Carvings of the Gothic Revival are not, like those of the Baroque, full of fun. But at least they can be good of their kind and are unfailingly safe. One supposes that the style is still surviving, and that, subject to modifications of fashion, it always will.

3. Proximate

WE COME now to questions connected with the Christian sculpture of our own time: how to judge it, how to improve it, how (if we are ourselves carvers) to go about it. In trying to meet such problems we must have at the back of our minds certain basic assumptions without which we shall be thrashing out in too many directions to allow for a conclusion. Unless we understand what Christian sculpture stands for, we cannot even begin either to judge, improve, or profitably work at it.

In order to pass judgment upon a work of Christian art, we must appreciate its direction. Christian art has a specific destination, and if we confuse this specific destination with any other we are in no position to pronounce upon the work. It is its final purpose which gives to the work its proper character as something religious and Christian. It is also its final purpose which determines the quality of its beauty. While every object of beauty that results from the work of man is a reflection of God's absolute beauty, those objects which are called religious and Christian must reflect God's beauty in a particular way.

If it is to qualify as a work of sacred art, then, the object must be directed: ultimately towards God, immediately towards the service of religion. If it is further to qualify as beautiful, it must reveal a concern more with absolute than with relative beauty. The first point proposes a straightforward issue: does the artist mean or not mean his work to follow the religious course? The conditions imposed upon his work by an affirmative answer to this question will be considered in a later chapter. Not so straightforward are the issues raised by the second point, and it is with these that we must now deal.

Since man's knowledge of absolute beauty is necessarily very limited, is normally less developed than his knowledge of relative beauty, is more interior and subtle than the knowledge which comes to him through the senses, the tendency will be to judge all beauty by relative—that is by natural, emotional, personal, sensible—standards. What follows will be an attempt not to teach absolute beauty—because nobody can *teach* beauty—but to indicate the approach to it. If even relative beauty cannot be strictly taught, at least some of the errors regarding it can be exposed.

Misconception in this matter of beauty derives mostly from the fact that all day long we are surrounded by natural, physical, intelligible things which, either favourably or adversely, are related to it. All the time we are picking out the agreeable and rejecting the disagreeable. Experiencing beauty at many different levels and in many different departments, we assume not only that the same rules can be applied indiscriminately but that we are free to make up the rules according to the dominant impression. We refer the data provided by one lot of perceptions to reactions which are stirred by a quite different lot of stimuli. Our guide is instinctively our own experience, the validity of which is measured by either the clarity or the intensity of the impression which it leaves behind.

We are apt, therefore, to judge works of art not by anything intrinsic to the works themselves but by the effects which they have on us. If the effects were always according to right reason, this system of judging would be fair enough. But since this is not normally the case, we tend to judge works of art by our favourite emotion, our acutest perception, our vividest memory. Thus we admire a statue because it reminds us of the crib at home, because it looks like someone we know, because it fits nicely into that awkward space, because it does not break when we knock it over. The only way to approach art is to approach it in its own terms, and in its own *essential* terms—as related to *essential* beauty.

Just as intellectual beauty differs from physical

beauty, as infant differs from adult and as spiritual differs from moral, so artistic beauty differs from natural or any other beauty. And until all terrestrial beauty finds its realization in eternal beauty, each separate beauty has its own separate laws. What all this is leading up to is that it is no good applying the laws of natural beauty to works which take their stand on sculptural beauty.

Not only is each order of creation governed by its own laws of beauty, but each order of art is governed by its own laws of beauty. The principles of the ballet may not be imposed upon straight acting, the principles of the film may not be imposed upon the puppet-show —still less upon painting and carving. This is something which is not infrequently forgotten, even by the artists themselves.

When an art-form neglects its proper laws, it loses its sense of material: it tends to imitate the expressions not only of nature but of other art-forms. Thus it will be considered an achievement when a piano is made to reproduce the sound of drops of rain upon a metal roof, when an organ can convey the twittering of birds (or the sighing of wind in the trees or a carillon of bells), when a flute brings out the notes which you would have thought could be rendered only by a double-bass. It is significant that when the violin was found capable of imitating exactly the sound of sawing wood, the

II. *Altar-Piece,* 5 ft. 3 in.

III.
Deposition,
5 ft.

IV.
Saint Joseph,
4 ft. 6 in.

V. *Head of Saint Martin*, 1 ft.

VI. *Saint Joseph and Child* (fragment)

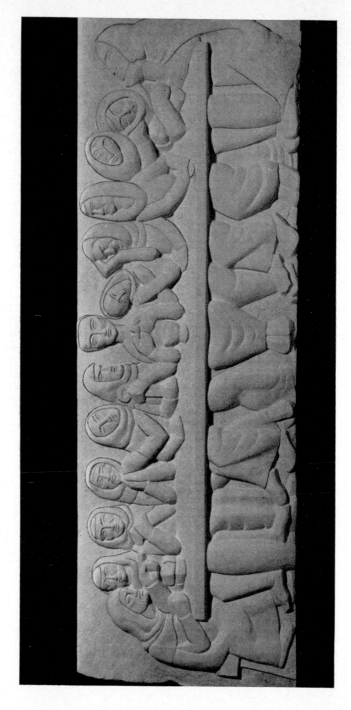

VII. *The Last Supper*, 10 ft. by 3 ft.

VIII. *Saint Thomas* (detail of *The Last Supper*)

IX. *Mary as a Child*

X.

Madonna and Child,
4 ft. 6 in.

XI. *Blessed Oliver Plunkett*, 2 ft. 6 in.

XII. *Abraham and Isaac* (unfinished), almost life-size

XIII.
Saint Benedict,
5 ft.

carpenter's saw was found hardly less capable of imitating the violin. This is called the law of aesthetic retaliation.

Nor, in this matter of judging art's proper beauty, is St. Thomas much help. When he says of created beauty that it is "that which gives pleasure on sight,"[1] he is felt to be begging the question. His, as M. Maritain points out, is a determination by *effect*. What we want determined for us is not so much the effect as the essence and the immediate cause. But it must be remembered that St. Thomas's words were not intended to be a definition; they were more in the nature of an aside. St. Thomas was anyway not greatly concerned with art—nowhere among his writings can be found a reference to a painting or a carving—so was simply stating the consequence of "conformity to that which should be." For the same reason, namely that the consequences are found to register differently in different people, we can never hope to find a cut-and-dried documentary formula which will put us right for good in our aesthetic appreciation. There are plenty to choose from,[2] but none gets us much nearer than

[1] *Id quod visum placet;* that which, being seen, pleases. (I.q. 5; art. 4, i.)

[2] "That is beautiful which gives pleasure for its own sake." (Kant) "Beauty is goodness in so far as this causes delight when it is known by the intellect." (Kleutgen, S. J.) "That which is in itself perfect is beautiful in so far as by reason of

Aeschylus's chorus in the *Agamemnon,* "my intestines do not lie" (σπλάγχνα δ'οὔτι ματᾴζει). The trouble about intestines is that they often *do* lie, especially when dictated to by the emotions.

While instinctive taste may take a man far on the way in the assessment of works of art, it cannot take him all the way. What is there to prove that his taste is right? It frequently happens that the intuitive appreciation is, in the light of certain objective canons, proved to have been justified. But in the valuation of aesthetic significance there must be more than the *Einfühlungs-heit*[3] which an occasional success has verified. If there is to be insight into the content of the work of art, if the importance of the work is to be measured according to the absolute standard proposed above, there must be principle in the approach. Even the principle of rejecting false principles of approach is something.

---

its perfection it is pleasing to our intellectual perception, and in consequence affords mental delight." (Stöckl) "The beauty of things is their intrinsic goodness in so far as by reason of this goodness they are fitted to be an object of delight to intellectual beings." (Jungmann, S. J.) More significant than these, because more objective, are Plato's and St. Augustine's definitions, which speak of beauty as the "splendour" of truth and the "splendour" of order. In the *De pulcro et bono,* ascribed to St. Albert the Great, beauty is taken to be the "splendour" or "brightness" of form appearing in the "well-proportioned elements of matter."

[3] Hunchmanship.

ii

The false approach most commonly employed is of course that of wanting works of art to resemble works of nature. It is certainly true that some of the work done both in stone and bronze by the greatest masters —Donatello, Michelangelo, Rodin, Mestrovic—has been naturalistic, but it is not because such work resembled nature that it was good sculpture. Not only did those particular objects possess other more important qualities besides that of naturalism but those particular masters produced other works which were not naturalistic. Naturalism by itself is no proof of excellence in a carving. More often than not it is a distinct handicap, distracting from the main intimation.[4]

Art may be taught of nature, *natura artis magistra,* but this does not mean that the pupil must look like the master. In the Christian sculpture of the fourteenth century nature was replacing the symbol. Until then,

[4] "The use of living models, except merely for reference, is a very great danger; for the beauties of appearance seek to oust the beauties of thought, and concern for accuracy of anatomical representation tends to oust concern for the beauty of the work itself. What is important is what the workman has in his mind, not what some model has in his body. This is the attitude of mind of all the great periods of sculpture: not what they saw but what they loved, that they carved. Truly they loved what they saw, but their seeing bent before their love as a sapling before the wind."—Gill, *Sculpture,* pp. 21, 22.

nature had been the index to be looked up when carving got stuck; the idea that *likeness* should be the main concern would have surprised the sculptors of the earlier schools. When the humanists, with their novel interpretation of reality, put nature in the first place, the symbolists went virtually out of business. But where you have a new concept of reality you have to invent new symbols to express it. So the idea of the symbol never quite went out.

For the sculptor who has undertaken to carve or model a portrait there is clearly an obligation to aim at some sort of likeness. But portraiture is only a branch, and a small branch, of carving; and even here the stone face is not meant to resemble absolutely the face of flesh and blood. The character of the stone or clay has to be expressed as well as the character of the sitter. The sitter's individuality will to a certain extent be expressed, unless the portrait is no more than a photograph in relief, by symbols.

On plate IV there appears what is meant to be a carpenter's saw. It will be seen to have the structure of an ordinary saw but the character of a stone saw. That is to say, it is the symbol of a saw conveyed in the medium of stone. (The question here is not whether it is well or badly done, but simply what it is.) Thus its serrated edge is meant to repeat the rhythm of the beard; its flat surface is meant to act as a wall keeping the rather loose figure compact and within bounds; its pronounced handle is meant to support the line of the hand. The saw is not designed to cut wood or make the sound of a violin.

The critic who complains "Why try to improve on nature?" has failed to grasp that between nature and sculpture there is no question of competition. The functions of each are entirely separate, and are connected not substantively but analogically. When God made man of flesh and blood he had in mind the range of activities, physical, intellectual, social and spiritual, which the human race would have to perform. A man would have to dig, build, raise a family, ride, write letters and ultimately fit bits of machinery together. The plan of man's body was designed to act humanly. But when a sculptor makes a man of stone he is presented with a quite different range of demand. The carved man has nothing to do in the way of human action so can be designed sculpturally. The carved man is primarily a symbol. All he has to do is to represent.

A carving is thus a re-presentation, a presentation anew, of something which may or may not bear resemblance to the original as presented by nature. There is all the difference between re-producing in a new mode of creative activity and reproducing likenesses to what has already been created. Where the former exercise considers the ideal, the divinely planned type, the latter exercise considers the actual examples resulting in the created order from the divine type. It is a question of orientation, and whenever sculpture is orientated towards realism it loses its sense of reality.

So the distinction has to be made in sculpture between what is real and what is realistic. Real sculpture need not be realistic, and realistic sculpture need not be real. What is known as "realism," "naturalism," "representationalism" is a danger to true sculpture in the measure that it demands the sacrifice of intrinsic to extrinsic values. Wherever sculpture's substantive good is replaced by an accidental good, you may get an advance in technological perfection, but you get a setback in Christian carving.

Realism, moreover, when carried beyond a certain point, defeats its own end. Representational sculpture, by inviting direct comparison with the object as found in nature, must inevitably be seen to fall short of nature's standards. The more idealized and symbolical the carving, the less is it likely to be held up against the natural type. Grinling Gibbons did no service to representational art, or to any other for the matter of that, when he carved vine leaves so delicately that, when painted and mounted on little hidden springs which caused them to rise and fall at a puff of wind, they were mistaken for real leaves. This was artistry,

not art. There is not much difference between artistry
and artifice. An artificial leaf, such as the factory-made
plastic variety which carries likeness to its extreme
limit, is in self-conscious rivalry with the real leaf.
The standard is too high: most would agree that nature's leaf is really better.

If Romanesque and Gothic carvers had wanted to
copy what they saw, they had the skill to do so. They
could have made marble drapery look like silk and
ivory wings look like feathers. But it was not what they
wanted to do. Instead they looked hard at drapery and
the wings of birds, and then interpreted what they saw.
By a process of abstraction and sculptural calculation
they found a convention for dealing with what they
saw. Then they forgot about what they had seen and
went to work on the new expression.

Ars imitatur naturam in sua operatione, says St.
Thomas:[5] "art copies nature by working as nature
works", *not* by copying the works of nature. Whenever
art steps outside its own proper way of working, it
falls into the error either of artistry, of artifice, or even
of anarchy. If art is, according to Rouault's definition,
"the conformity of the sensible world with a certain
interior light," it follows that where one or other—
either the sensible world or the interior light—refuses
to conform, the result is a negation of art. Take the

[5] I, q. 117; art. i.

sensible world as your final arbiter, and what happens? Your "certain interior light" clouds over and you get nothing but realism. Take the interior light as your final arbiter, and what happens? The "sensible world" recedes until you reach the impasse of abstraction. For true art there has to be conformity, equilibrium.

So between art, which is right relationship, and anarchy, which is its opposite, you find all those artistic substitutes which come about because the interior light is not quite strong enough to reveal the beauty of the sensible world, and because the manipulative ability is present to reproduce accurately the limited beauty which is seen. For example, our twentieth-century cult of eccentricity is a dangerous artistic substitute. The nineteenth-century cult of classicism was a dangerous substitute for an art which had lost its way in the emotion of Romanticism and the *chic* of Rococo. But perhaps more harmful to the course of true sculpture than these cults is the perennial cult of prettiness.

Cultivated ugliness in sculpture is bad enough, but cultivated prettiness is almost worse. Prettiness, just as truly as ugliness, is the enemy of the beautiful. In *L'Art*, Rodin describes how a great artist can pick up what the world calls ugly and turn it into something beautiful. To the great artist perhaps nothing is seen as wholly ugly. Certainly to pick up what is pretty and turn it into something beautiful requires genius. Donatello managed it. Michelangelo obviously never tried: the pretty did not interest him. The pretty must have appealed to Della Robbia because it appears in most of his work, and he seems to have made no attempt to transform it. There was undoubtedly much prettiness in the subjects chosen by the Flemish artists, who, in their best period, transformed it into beauty. The French often rose from the pretty to the beautiful— more in their Gothic than in their later styles—but just as often remained pledged to prettiness. The famous eighteenth-century French sculptor Houdon, looked up to even by Rodin, appears to have been undecided as to what was pretty and what was beautiful. He would carve in the strong and model in the weak, attracted mainly by the commonplace—which he rendered with great fidelity. But Houdon's work is always interesting, if only because it stands out from that of his contemporaries, who must have been dancing-masters. In our own time, Rosandic, master of technique and composition, has shown himself (witness his *La Pucelle*) to be the supreme exponent of sculptured prettiness.

So far as England is concerned, it is difficult to generalize on this point: English carving has apparently framed no policy. For Gill, at any rate, surface charm had no meaning whatever: never has there been a sculptor who made fewer concessions. Epstein,

who can with equal facility turn ugly things into beautiful and beautiful into ugly, quotes Modigliani as calling
the sculptor of skin-deep loveliness *un faiseur de
beauté*.

Especially in religious carving must the quality of
attractiveness be backed by qualities more authentic.
The critic as well as the sculptor should know that the
kind of good looks which are admired on the stage are
not the kind of good looks which are to be expected
from the stone. If the fairness of a celebrated beauty
is not the fairness of a carved Venus, still less is it the
fairness of a carved saint. Again it is the fallacy of "likeness"—likeness to a type extrinsic to the proper craft.
The first thing a stone beauty has to look like is stone.

iii

We have reached this far in our examination of appreciation: we know that when a man's first thought
on seeing a work of sculpture is "How cleverly contrived" or "How enchanting" he is either not in the
presence of true sculpture or else not looking for the
right thing. It is not the function of sculpture to elicit
speculation upon the method employed, the materials
used, the identity of the artist. It is not the function of
sculpture to elicit gasps of surprise, waves of nostalgia,
transports of grief. All these things are by-products.
The primary appeal of sculpture is direct. The response
to sculpture should be correspondingly direct.

It is a curious fact that in this matter of passing judgment on a piece of sculpture the ordinary man will assume a right to pronounce where in other fields he would acknowledge his incapacity. Few men, for example, without training and experience, would claim to know better than the wrestler, the surgeon, the chef, the judge. It is about the visual arts, evidently, that every man is possessed of an infused knowledge. In the case of literature it is less surprising that a man should say categorically of a book that it is well or badly written: he has himself written letters and he knows what the written sentence is supposed to do. But a man will judge a carving who for the life of him could not draw a nose.

Another curious fact is that whereas in other fields the process of translating one reality into another is understood by all—nobody expects an aeroplane to look like a bird or a submarine to look like a fish—in the field of art there is this hankering after fidelity to a known type. No one sitting down to breakfast is heard to complain that his fried egg no longer resembles the egg as it was in its natural state when it left the hen, that his bacon no longer resembles the pig that was killed for eating. People assume that a process of rearrangement has taken place in which the natural mode of being has been left behind. It is not that the natural has been judged by the man responsible for the rearrangement as in any way inferior: it is just that the man's job being what it was (it might be the cook's job, as in the above example, but it might be equally, *mutatis mutandis*, the gardener's, the carpenter's, the shoemaker's, the hairdresser's) a new articulation (or shape, or expression) has been given to the existing material.

If people allowed to sculptors the liberty which they allow to other craftsmen in the common work of transposition, they might be less ready to plunge into the arena of criticism. This is not to suggest that only the professional has a right to express an opinion. It is merely to suggest that those who do express their opinions are not always the best qualified to do so. While the people who are known as the general public have every right to say what kind of sculpture they like, the people who are known as the professionals have every right to expect reasons for the preference.

Since the general public must necessarily exert a considerable influence upon sculpture (we are thinking particularly of Christian sculpture) it would be both unwise and unethical for the professionals to dismiss its opinion out of hand. Unwise, because in the long run the public is going to get what it wants. Unethical, because to stand aloof from the thought of the many, where it is a question of neither faith nor morals, is to commit the sin of pride.

For the sculptor and spectator alike it is worth noting that the appreciation of sculpture is not quite on a par with the appreciation of other art-forms. The reasons for this are partly practical and partly psychological. From the practical point of view there are fewer carved objects to be studied than there are pictures to be seen, books to be read, musical sounds to be heard. The average citizen is seeing pictures in one form or another from morning to night: illustrated papers, advertisements, photographs, portraits and landscapes. He is constantly making judgments upon them and arriving at some sort of principle about their composition. As regards other art-forms the same process is unconsciously going on: the citizen is building up, not very consciously perhaps, a collection of canons, comparative standards, predilections and prejudices. The number of books which he reads in the year is probably greater than the number of statues which he looks at. He goes more often to the theatre than he goes to an exhibition of sculpture. Music comes out of the radio, sculpture does not. The citizen has to go out of his way to find carvings which are going to help him in his approach to the question of sculpture, Christian or other.

In the nature of the case, carvings are more scarce than most other objects of art because they come from a more unwieldy material. Statues take time to make, and are not so easy to move about as most artistic expressions. The result is that the general public, until pressed to give an opinion on it, or shocked by some more violent manifestation of it, is largely indifferent to sculpture, is largely unaware of it. So when the general public goes to church and finds itself surrounded with religious images, or when the general public for social or commemorative reasons finds itself in the presence of unavoidable civic sculpture, the principles of sculptural assessment are lacking.

Instead of saying simply and humbly, "I don't know; I really cannot judge; please explain," the general public is suddenly fired with the desire to pass sentence. The judgment is given as infallible and final. Pretending to no education in the matter, the general public writhes in its complex of artistic inferiority. No wonder it voices its feelings—which are the sole criterion— with a certain bluster. Our argument is that if there were more sculpture and better sculpture which the general public could see, there would be less reliance upon feelings as the sole criterion. Our argument is, further, that because the best periods of sculpture (in our opinion the earliest) are the least accessible, the general public labours under the practical disadvantage of not knowing where to look.

The second, and psychological, reason why the understanding of sculpture is not on a level with other appreciations is that it seems to develop later in a person's life than the rest. We are considering here the feeling for sculpture as a serious interest. A child may, and indeed normally does, react instinctively and correctly to carved objects. The child reacts in the same way to painted pictures. But in the case of most people there is a period between childhood and maturity when sculpture means nothing at all. During this gap a sense of prettiness is developed, and a new respect for the technical, the mechanical, the realistic, is awakened. If, as is held, the appreciation of painting undergoes a change during the years of adolescence, appreciation of sculpture is almost wholly submerged and for a longer time. When the young man wakes up to the possibilities of sculpture, he is earning his living or getting married or finding his artistic interests supplied adequately enough through other channels.

It is all very well to say that the solution to all these problems of appreciation lies in putting the case before people, showing them where to find the best examples of sculpture available, and telling them to get on with it. But the education of taste is not so easy as that. Taste depends upon the apprehension through the senses of something which lies beyond the senses. You cannot implant true and good taste as regards Christian sculpture unless the person in whom you are trying to plant it agrees with you about the true and the good. Unless there is an accepted foundation, a fulcrum, you cannot raise anything—however serviceable the lever. You might just as well try to raise yourself into the air by pulling on your socks.

Taste—by itself and without foundations—is an arbitrary quality. You may have it or you may not. The connoisseur has it and the roadmender has it not: but this is now expert knowledge and not strictly what we Christians would call taste. What we would call taste in the discernment of true Christian sculpture is that same quality which discerns the transcendent beauty of God reflected in his created world.

To this it will be objected that the serious art critic does not have to know about God before he can tell whether a piece of carving is good or not. Granted that he is no charlatan, may he not be looked to as an arbiter of sculptural and Christian taste? Within a limited and applied meaning of the terms he can indeed. The sincere critic who has no interest in the transcendental, who has no experience of prayer, who does not take our view of absolute beauty to be found in God alone, can judge just so far as his senses, his intelligence, his training, take him. You cannot expect him to know anything of the spiritual quality of the work—spiritual in our sense of the word, not merely "mysteriously elevating"—because he has nothing in his mind to which the spiritual quality can be related. If he pronounces upon the spiritual quality, he will be either guessing or meaning something else.

Therefore a man can judge true Christian sculpture only by sharing the mind of the sculptor who conceives it, and the sculptor can carve true Christian sculpture only by sharing the mind of Christ. You can talk about spirituality and absolute values only when your aspiration stretches beyond materialism and relative values. To spiritualize your work—whether it is the work of judging or of actually cutting stone—you must spiritualize your life and your desire.

So the only contribution, apart from seeing that the erroneous approaches are avoided, which one man may make towards another's education in the appreciation of sculpture lies in pointing so consistently at the ultimate realities that the other's mind is drawn to look in the same direction as his own. Never has the need for this sort of education been greater than in an age like the present when there are few fixed standards, few clear objectives to aim at. Where the supernatural is at a discount, the natural will be in confusion.

It was in this connection that Gill showed himself to be in the full sense a master: his disciples learned not only to carve in his way but to think in his way. Where the ordinary leader of a fashion in sculpture is content to impose a convention and remove a misconception, the master directs positively the minds of others. He knows that the idea is the main thing, and that if this is got right the expression of the idea will follow. Gill, in his writing and carving alike, stood for the supernatural when even his Catholic contemporaries had no thought beyond the natural.[6]

So far, then, we have argued that while sculptural appreciation may be cultivated and confirmed by association with other minds it cannot be created by human agency where there exists a prejudice against the final cause and end. If nature abhors a vacuum, so also does art. But so long as it is only a vacuum, and not determination, there is hope. Since there are few who are genuinely incapable of reacting favourably to beauty in sculpture when its principles are pointed out to them, there is always the hope that people will come to react more and more favourably—coming eventually to the appreciation of uncreated beauty, divine beauty itself.

Thus what we might call the general-public difficulty lies not with the small minority of honest and admitted morons—the people who do not want to be helped towards aesthetic appreciation and who are quite happy to remain silent whenever the question of art is raised—nor yet with the people who suspect that their taste is bad but who are willing to take steps to improve it; the difficulty lies with those who have

[6] Unfortunately, as so often happens, the craftsmen who came after him continued Gill's mannerisms but neglected to continue his thinking—with the result that Catholic England is today littered with an off-Gill statuary wholly devoid of animation.

never taken the trouble to examine the primary tenets of art and who assume that their knowledge of all its branches is native to them. It is these last, often the majority in a society, who wield the influence. Native the appreciative faculty may once have been, but the early response has been overlaid, we must remember, with every sort of matter collected in the process of growing up in a world which is not given to stressing the postulates of either art or religion. Sciences which the world teaches, bringing new influences to bear upon the critical faculty, provide analogies which are close enough to suggest parallels, yet not close enough to be of any real use.

iv

Since the concrete case speaks more clearly than argument, I am venturing here to adopt the first person singular and to quote from experience. While working recently on *The Last Supper* (plate VII) I was visited by people of different ages and tastes. From the comments made by my visitors I select three which seemed to be significant. "I like those big strong men," said a little girl of five. Now though the carving is large (ten foot long) there is nothing in the drawing to indicate the size of the men. The figures are not big, for example, in relation to the table. Nor is there anything in the anatomy to suggest that they are meant to be powerful. So the child had caught from the stone the implications which I had hoped to convey. Hers was to me a gratifying comment. The other two were less so.

"The chalice doesn't look as if it is sitting on the table," said a boy of sixteen. He then added: "But I suppose it couldn't with the table at that angle; it would slip off." This was interesting because it showed that his standard was instinctively that of realism. He had forgotten his formalized plastic duck (as sculptural in principle as the work of John Skeaping) and the conventions which had governed the figures of Mr. and Mrs. Noah. He had lost the sense of roundness which had appealed to him about Humpty Dumpty. The combined effect of films, television, and "method" had obliterated the idea of a stylized Punch and Judy. In other words his emancipation had altered, unconsciously of course, his values. Through the false sculpture of realistic metal soldiers, and the still more realistic wax figures of Madame Toussaud's, the boy had come almost to judge as one of the general public. Almost, but not altogether. At least he had gathered from the composition that it was primarily eucharistic.

The third of the selected comments ran as follows: "The faces seem to me rather expressionless. But it must be very difficult to get people's expressions in stone. And anyway it appears to be the modern idea to make people's faces look blank." This came from a man of my own age, educated and in business: a citizen. There are several points to be noted about this astonishing and highly indicative statement. First it was of cardinal importance, evidently, that stone faces should show an emotion of some sort. Second it was only the unyielding nature of the material which could excuse from depicting expression. Third it could be taken as one of the aims of modern carving to intimate blankness. There speaks the voice of the general public—at its *kindest*.

Of the three visitors who commented on the carving, it is the third to whom I now find myself most indebted. The citizen's summing up has driven me back to a re-examination of the position, and a workman has constantly to overhaul his theory, or his work will show signs of staleness. What the citizen said has confirmed my suspicion that the face is the first, and very often the *only*, part of a statue which the general public looks at. The other two visitors were not immediately interested in faces but in impressions. What the general public does not realize is that the value of a carving does not depend upon the treatment of any one part. It is not a question of getting the facial expression right, and the rest will not be noticed. Rather it is a question of getting the whole sculptural composition right, and then it does not matter if the face is noticed or not. A statue does not stand or fall by a few square inches which lie between the base of the forehead and the line of the lower jaw: it stands or falls by every square inch related to every other.[7]

The citizen's further suggestion that emptiness of countenance was a device favoured by the moderns drove me again to a review both of my own period and of my own technique. *Do* the moderns prefer the vacant look? Or is it that they give blank faces to their statues because their own minds, failing to reflect reality, are blank? Am I for my part so much on my guard against romanticism in sculpture that my stone men stare vapidly into space? Or is it that we all of us in the trade try to convey emotion sculpturally and fail? I confess I do not know the answers to these questions. What I do know is that the general public no longer expects a work of sculpture to be an expression of praise to God.[8]

[7] Not unrelated to the above is Epstein's admission that the part of the human head which he finds the most difficult to model is the surface above the socket of the eyes. The features, nose and ears and mouth, give him less trouble. He can always get roundness out of the features. It is where there are no marked features, as in the forehead, that the shape of the skull needs all the more careful attention. This information, incidentally, is not given in *The Sculptor Speaks,* so can be vouched for only by hearsay.

[8] It may be of interest to add that among the many visitors who called while I was at work it was never the young who asked why I had not carved fingers and toes. It was only their seniors who were bothered by this.

v

While we complain about the lack of appreciation today in the matter of sculpture, particularly in the matter of religious sculpture, we forget that the whole business of appreciation must have been very much simpler in the ages of the faith. On an earlier page we have noted how, when the workmen and the people for whom they work are agreed about God, the work corresponds to the conviction. So where public and professionals alike are agreed on the fundamentals of faith, there is less room for disagreement in the judgment of works which are related to those fundamentals. In a society where there is little unity regarding religion, and where there is is no general recognition of the relationship between art and religion, the standard of appreciation, because its evaluations are dissipated, will be low.

The west country peasants and rural townsmen who stood watching while the front of Wells Cathedral or Bath Abbey was under construction would have seen the carvings in their wider context. The cut stone was to them part of a pattern which was more important than the designer's drawings. It was not that they knew their history better than the men of Somerset know it today and were able to trace an ancestry to the style of carving in front of them; it was not that they knew their Bible better than the men of Somerset know it today and were able to see the scriptural references in the sculptural representation. What they knew better was their faith.

But we must not make the mistake of romanticizing this. We do not have to conclude that the medieval man enjoyed the blessing of good taste in virtue of his Christian baptism. Nor need we imagine that the general public in earlier periods swallowed new manifestations in sculpture with any better grace than do their counterparts today. Contemporary sculpture has probably produced a sundering effect in every generation, dividing craftsman from citizen and even craftsman from craftsman. If contemporary work is alive at all, and not regressive, it is bound to be controversial. People in England during the fourteenth century were almost certainly asking why these wretched modern carvers, with their everlasting crowns and smiles and high waists and affected postures could not go on shaping stone as those nice Normans had shaped it for goodness knew how long. It is a pretty safe bet that the Normans in their turn were complained of in the England of the twelfth century as being uncouth innovators. "Why not let us keep up the old Celtic style which was good enough for our fathers and grandfathers? Geometric designs and a few formal plants and animals are far more dignified than all these

people which they seem to want in sculpture now."
And so on, back into antiquity. And always tagging
along in the train of each successive movement there
is the little bunch of intellectuals who, although they
may be perfectly right, are bringing discredit upon
the whole thing. So it is classed highbrow to appreciate
both the extremely ancient and the extremely progressive schools, lowbrow to appreciate the more conservative. The archaic is canonized by the few and
misinterpreted by the many; the conservative is taken
as standard and reproduced to death; the contemporary is controversial. Philistia, Philistia, what hast thou
not refused?

Thus our argument moves in a circle. If you do not
see much of a thing, you do not as a rule see deeply
into that thing. Where in the ages of the faith men saw
true sculptural things all round them, men of our own
age have to visit a museum in order to look at an icon.[9]
A thing which you do not understand becomes one
which you will want to belittle. The understanding of
Christian sculpture comes from seeing into it, not from
glancing over it. "Without the inspiration of a personal
or at least of a national faith," writes Mr. Ramsden,
who certainly has no Catholic axe to grind, "that *living*
quality by which even the most commonplace things

[9] Englishmen and Americans are willing enough to visit
museums, but not in their own countries.

may be dignified must be wanting. Modern ideologies based on conceptions of the *rights* of man are not enough. 'There is no God,' cry the masses . . . and with the loss of God, man loses his sense of values."[10] The writer goes on to describe how Mestrovic, when asked what he thought was most lacking in the students of sculpture today, replied: "C'est une qualité d'âme qui manque." Mr. Ramsden and Mestrovic are here epitomizing the causes not only of our sculptural weakness but of our weakness as a civilized race. It is faith held in common that gives common supernatural standards by which to evaluate current politics, science, education, philosophy, life itself. If the Christian of the Middle Ages did not have to bother as we do about questions of aesthetic appreciation, it was because he possessed the answers to most of them along with his religious conviction.

Looked at from the other way round, it might be said that if all men agreed to follow materialism absolutely, and to express it in every work of their hands, the question of artistic appreciation would again, as in the case of the Middle Ages, be vastly simplified. But there are rival cultures at work, and the men of our time are never wholly committed. When each man feels free to propose to himself his own god, he is not likely to agree with the next man about what gives

[10] *Sculpture: Theme and Variations,* p. 4.

glory to *any* god. Having lost one common faith, man has found no other to replace it. Hardly surprising that his appreciations are all at sea, and that he cannot understand what art is all about.

4. More Proximate

HAVING tried to find a way of judging Christian sculpture, we must now try to find a way of promoting it. If Christian sculpture is to be promoted at all, and not simply left to reiterate itself in dead forms, the impulse must come from three sources at once: from the priest, from the layman, from the man who cuts the stone. It is a curious fact that however scornful he may be about the trends of sculpture in his generation, the priest will nevertheless want to have statues of some sort in his church. The layman in the same way will want to worship where there are carvings of the saints to look at. The sculptor exists to supply what is needed. Only where the three are ready to act with spirit and in unison can there be a progressive Christian sculpture.

If the feeling for sculpture is today weak within the Church, and compared with other ages it is very weak indeed, the fault is not so much the Church's, the layman's, the craftsman's: the fault is in the lack of interaction. The Church fails to give a lead, the laity lose interest, and the sculptors go their own way. While it would be an impertinence to claim more than the evidence of history entitles us to claim, we can say nevertheless that such a situation is relatively new.[1]

"The history of western art," writes one of the most eminent of Catholic artists, Jean Charlot, "was long synonymous with that of the Church. The Church was the most active patron of artists, and all flocked naturally to her. Time was when a pope, picking an adolescent out of a crowd of applicants, found his reward in a Sistine Chapel or Raphael's Stanzas. Today, the link between artists and Church that in the past worked wonders seems severed. The Church today is an uncertain patron, fallen from its great estate as appreciator of untried styles; the Church is also an irascible patron, quick to suspect the new, its memory of the art revolutions that it once consistently helped, lost. The artist is still at work, painting ways of the cross and flights into Egypt, only to put them eventually in storage; carving statues worthy of God's house, only to leave them behind to avoid freight charges on moving day. The cleric now shops for church art not where he would naturally find it, in the artist's studio, but more conveniently in the rectory, from the mail-order

---

[1] It may be well to say that when the action of the Church is mentioned here and elsewhere in this book, various degrees of authority and importance are involved.

catalogue. What aesthetic junk he buys as a result will visually foul his church, debase the piety of his parishioners into pietistic routines, and be seized upon by the gleeful unbeliever as another proof that the Church is indeed in its decadence."[2]

Without the Church's backing, which means more than reluctant sanction, the layman and the artist can do nothing to further the cause of Christian sculpture. Though artists may make bad prelates, and prelates may make bad artists, there is no reason why prelate and artist should not work together for the glory of God in Christian sculpture and for the edification of the layman. "The vocation of the creative liturgical artist has become so fiercely impractical today," says Jean Charlot in the same article, "that it must be more than ever a tried way, if a trying one, of serving God." The way is tried and trying, not because of the nature of the vocation but because of the nature of the frustration which it meets with from above and from the side.

Sculptors are not by profession martyrs, and after a while—and under such pressures as indifference, discouragement, seeing inferior factory-made products winning in the competition every time—they give up. A sculptor has a right to live, and even, if he can, to get rich. It is very easy for him to throw his carving principles to the winds and to become himself a fac-

[2] *Liturgical Arts,* November 1958, p. 23.

tory, turning out what priest and public seem to want. The sculptor's responsibility, however, both as a craftsman and as a Catholic, will be considered in the next chapter.

It is here, in the matter of the ecclesiastical impetus to be given to sculpture, that the religious orders might be more of a help than they are. Not so much in providing schools of religious sculpture—though that too —as in providing an uncompromising example and a positive policy: this is where the monastery can act with greater freedom than the parish. In the case of the monastery the argument does not hold that the wishes of the uninitiated must be met. There is also in the religious life more opportunity than in the seminary of studying the principles of aesthetics, and for linking them up with liturgical worship. Where the religious orders are found to give a forthright lead, the laity as well as the diocesan clergy can confidently be expected to follow.

In fact it might be argued that the best people to engage themselves in religious art are the religious, that the people most likely to lead a return to liturgical sculpture are those most pledged to the liturgy. While this may be true, it should be pointed out that there are practical drawbacks to the idea of monks and friars becoming professional religious sculptors and educators in Christian art. Since each religious order has its own particular work to attend to, art can hardly be more than a side-line. Those dedicated to preaching or teaching cannot well spare the time, and their communities cannot well spare the subjects, for such a specialized occupation as sculpture. Sculpture for a religious can never be more than an occupation within a vocation; it cannot, as it can in the case of the layman, become a vocation in itself.[3]

Within such limits and given such conditions, might it not be possible to extend to sculpture the work which is being done with success in several Benedictine abbeys in England—pottery and stained glass at Buckfast, weaving at Downside, pottery and woodengraving and painting at Prinknash?[4] Or perhaps a group of Oblates could be persuaded to affiliate them-

[3] Also, for the older orders anyway, the absence from the monastery of monks following a course of training at an artschool is undesirable. Greater freedom would be possible in the case of laybrothers, who are not only less tied to the liturgical time-table in the monastery but are in any event liable for apprenticeship of some sort. Training in the manual trade of sculpture is as good as any. Nor is training in the work of painting to be despised by the laybrother. Fra Angelico was a laybrother.

[4] At Stanbrook Abbey sculpture is well represented by the work of Dame Werburg Welch. Dame Werburg, whose reliefs in wood are models of composition and true spiritual sensibility, ranks high above any other religious, monk or nun, carving in England today.

selves to a community with the particular end in view of furthering sacred sculpture. There are obvious drawbacks to this scheme too, but they are not insuperable. Where art-folk are concerned there will always be drawbacks.

ii

In addition to the responsibility of giving encouragement to sculpture, the Church has the responsibility of trusting the sculptor. The Church must give to the craftsman the credit of knowing his job. Assuming that the craftsman is a member of the faithful, the Church must further give to him the credit of wanting to serve God and his fellow faithful. The fact that the Church can count upon the craftsman's obedience does not entitle churchmen to turn craftsmen into slaves.

If sculpture is to advance along Christian lines, there has to be collaboration in charity, and this means reciprocal concessions as well as reciprocal trust. Nothing can be done if collaboration gives place to the relationship of domination and servitude. While it is true that an arrogant sculptor is sometimes in the position of laying down the law to cowed ecclesiastics, it is far more often the case that ecclesiastical authorities dictate terms to the sculptor. And very understandably so, since it is the clergy who are paying for the work.

What each side has to remember is that the glory of

God is the common aim, and that the work to be produced will be determined by qualities relating precisely to this. In producing the work, the sculptor must
be allowed to preserve his own inalienable identity.
A subject of the Church, a member of Christ's mystical
body, the sculptor remains a person in his own right.

The sculptor himself and those commissioning the
work must alike accept, as far as it goes, the analogy
from creation. Where God creates out of nothing, man
creates out of something. The parallel therefore is not
complete: the action in man's case is not properly that
of creating but that of fashioning. There is an affinity
nevertheless, even a sort of complicity, between the
creative act of God and the creative act of man. As
God breathes into the human being a separate spirit,
a likeness of his own spirit, so the sculptor breathes
into his stone a separate spirit which is a likeness of
his own.

The sculptor is "creating" in the sense that something
exists outside himself which had hitherto existed only
in his own mind. Though the new entity is no more
than the shape given to a substance already there, the
act which conceives and produces the shape is properly analogous to that which conceives and produces
the works of creation. So it follows that every work
produced by the art of man is unique. If it is not
unique, but one like a hundred others, it is without

character. Bearing the character of its author, the work has an individuality which no outside power should seek to eliminate. A design must come out from a man's own head, and his work must come out from a man's own hands. And this must be understood by the people who are employing him.

From the sculptor's point of view, the work remains with him all his life. Like an indiscretion, it cannot be wholly shaken off. It can be sold or forgotten or lost, but it cannot belong essentially (again like an indiscretion) to someone else. It can become the property of someone else, but it remains begotten of the sculptor's vision. A slave may be owned by another man, but he goes on being the son of his father.

From the proprietor's point of view, the work may not be mutilated to suit his own taste. The mere fact that a man has paid a just price for a piece of sculpture does not entitle him to take it home and alter it. The proprietor, if he thinks that the work needs changing (and if the sculptor is still alive), has the duty of consulting the person who, because he was in on it from the beginning and it was he who directed its development, must know more about the particular work than anyone else.

You would say that decency demands as much. Yet how often will you not find that in the interests of edification or the prevailing fashion a piece of carving has been adapted by a hand not the carver's? In an age which delights in making digests of the classics, in making musicals out of straight plays, in "basing" film scripts on the original text, we may expect to see a lot more of this.

iii

As a pendant to the above there is another factor which, though not so serious as either putting sculptors out of work by neglecting them in favour of the machine or hacking their carvings about when the contract has been fulfilled, can have a stultifying influence on the stone-cutting trade. If sculpture is to serve the Church, and if the Church is to do its duty by sacred sculpture, carved work must be suitably placed. By putting statues in the wrong setting, the patron can reduce their effectiveness by about half.

Since the question of placing modern figures in ancient churches and ancient figures in modern churches is a living one, a sense of congruity is of some importance. Without such a sense there can result only a clash of styles which will not only upset the artistic harmony but also distract the faithful in their worship. Where a piece of sculpture fights with its background or with other objects of sculpture, the impression will be one of restlessness. There are two things to notice about this. First, it is not always their fault that carvings clash with their surroundings—indeed if their surroundings are bad, it is a matter of merit that they do. Second, the purer the style of carving the readier will it mix. At a time like the present, when both religious sculpture and religious architecture are tending towards simplification, these are points to be borne in mind.

It is no criticism of Mestrovic's *Deposition* to say that it lacks the note of congruity in the Gothic Revival surroundings of the collegiate church at South Bend, Indiana, where in any case it is very difficult to see. Nor is a *Madonna* of Gill's to blame for being out of place in a garden grotto a few miles from Drogheda in Southern Ireland, where (when the sun shines) it can be seen only too well. In its restored Tudor environment, again, the Henry Moore figure at Dartington Hall strikes a false note. In each case there is nothing wrong with the carving, which would mix well enough if it were given half a chance, but in the attempted combination. The patrons have been right in their choice of object but wrong in their choice of position.

More marked sometimes than the clash of religious styles is the clash of religious spirits. Bernini's *Saint Teresa in Ecstasy* is spiritually out of tune with the church of S. Maria della Vittoria. Bernini masterpieces are more for showrooms than churches. Sir Ninian Comper's *Saint Joan,* though devoutly conceived and efficiently executed, is spiritually out of tune with Winchester Cathedral. It would do better on the prow of a sailing vessel—a sailing vessel with a crew of girl guides. Lacking in spiritual as well as sculptural congruity is the Egyptian monolith which, standing sentinel before the church door, serves as a war memorial in a parish in South Wales.

All of which suggests that carvings should be designed for the sites which they will occupy. Religious statues—like the buildings of Mr. Frank Lloyd Wright which seem to grow out of the rocks, out of the plains, out of the streets—should look as though they had come up through the floor of the church and had grown into the life of the place.

It does not follow from this that architecture and statuary must be kept rigidly to the same period, but it does follow that the two must belong to the same interpretation. One of the encouraging signs about the trends of the present day is that the more direct interpretation of Byzantine and Romanesque art is found to go better with modern buildings than any of the later styles. It is possible that people will draw conclusions from this.

For so long as those who buy statues buy them at random ("We're sure to find a place to put it"), there can be no direction about the good which they propose. For as long as those who make statues neglect to follow them up ("It's their job to see that it's in a

decent light"), the communication between sculptor
and patron and spectator is obscured. The work has a
right to be seen at advantage, placed at the right
height, freed from shadows thrown by other objects,
uncramped by buttresses or ceiling, and even if necessary floodlit or painted. The workman has a duty to
see that reasonably good conditions are secured. There
is only this qualification to be made: the work must
be shown according to its nature.

Thus if the lighting effects, or the polychromatic
finish which is given to the work, or the introduction
of different textures and materials—if any extrinsic
element—will produce an articulation foreign to the
character of sculpture, there is no justification for such
devices. Sculpture is for something more than to supply
a *coup de théatre.* The faithful may clamour for such
tricks, and the clergy may join in the clamour, but if
the sculptor allows himself to be pushed about by the
common demand for what he feels to be inferior art he
is finished as a sculptor. He has allowed himself to be
absorbed into the materialist machine; he has sold himself, and will produce nothing more that is worth a
second glance.

iv

We have now considered our subject from the angle
of the stone, of history, and of theory; we have also
considered it from the more personal angle of the ec-

clesiastical patron, the interested layman, and the professional craftsman. It is time we considered the approach to Christian sculpture from the angle of the Church.

Since we cannot expect the Church to help on something of which she does not approve, we must find out how far the Church approves of contemporary movements in sculpture and how much she is committed to their support. As members of the Church we have the duty of trying to see sculpture as the Church sees it, of helping it in the way that the Church wants it helped.

While there has been no definitive pronouncement from Rome about modern trends in sculpture, enough can be gathered from the encyclical *Mediator Dei* of 1947 and the *Instructio de Arte Sacra* of 1952 to see the direction of the Church's thought. In both documents the liturgy is presented as the "major art" in which all other arts inhere "as the liturgy's very noble servants." The encyclical warns against excessive symbolism on the one hand and excessive naturalism on the other. Exaggeration in either direction, insisted the Holy Father, was more likely to manifest itself in the case of the plastic than in the case of the other arts. It is clear from the text that greater uneasiness is felt about sculpture than about architecture, and though no reason is given for this, the explanation is fairly obvious: areas enclosed by walls and ceiling have a less direct effect upon people's minds than the carved objects which they see within those areas.

The liturgy, then, is taken to be the key to the whole thing. It is also the yardstick by which the carvings themselves are measured. The Christian church is the earthly dwelling of God's presence where the faithful are prepared by that presence for the place which they will occupy in the eternal dwelling of heaven. Christian iconography furnishes that church with reference to the same end. If a house, to quote Le Corbusier's famous dictum, is a "machine to live in," a church is a machine to get ready for heaven in.

Since it is the liturgy, finding its climax in the sacrifice of the Mass, which not only gets people ready for heaven but is the primary and appropriate activity to be performed within the walls of a church—the masonry being built round the liturgy—it will be the liturgy which gives the note to the statues, decoration, arrangement. The liturgy is not merely the noise which the machine makes when it is lived in and prayed in; it is the power of the machine and the essential *ratio* of each mechanical part.

The encyclic idea that sculpture is one of the "very noble servants" which minister to the "major art" of liturgical worship must be correctly understood if either the sculptural or the liturgical movement is to be advanced. "This is a very suggestive symbol indeed," comments Dom Frédéric Debuyst, "but it must not, we think, go beyond this. In intellectualizing it too much, we would run the risk either of drawing liturgy towards aesthetics, which would be bad theology (for liturgy is a directly and essentially religious reality, hence much *more* than a thing of aesthetical experience), or else of elaborating a non-aesthetic philosophy of art, which would be very imprudent, not to say absurd."[5] The subject which Dom Debuyst opens up is beyond the scope of the present study; the alternative extremes, however, which he foresees as the possible consequences of the doctrine are much to the point and to be guarded against.

When we turn from the encyclical and the *Instructio* to the pastorals of bishops and to the statements made by various authoritative representatives of the Church, we find much the same direction of thought. Bishop Agostini, for example, when regulating for the building of churches in the diocese of Padua, is ready "to accept the new but not the eccentric." Mgr. Anichini, canon of St. Peter's in Rome and lecturer on the history of art, takes his stand on the ruling published by the *Pontefice Accademia dei Virtuosi del Pantheon,* which runs: "Painting and sculpture in modern sacred art may be carried out with greater simplicity of tech-

[5] "The Present Problem of Sacred Art," *Art d'Eglise,* no. 105; 4e trimestre, 1958.

nique, in a more synthetic and stylistic manner, and with profounder modelling of nature; but it must avoid absolutely aridity and deformed caricature."

The difficulty about each of the above citations is that words like "eccentric," "arid," "deformed" mean different things to different people. Even in the case of *Mediator Dei*, which is more explicit, the point at which sane art leaves off and mad art begins is not altogether clear. The relevant passage is as follows: "We cannot but deplore those images recently introduced which seem a deformation of sane art, which are repugnant alike to dignity, modesty, and Christian piety, and which deeply wound the religious sense."[6] A final quotation from *Mediator Dei* will show that, for all its strictures, it is not the Church's policy to stifle the contemporary in sacred art: "We must absolutely leave the field open for the art of our times when it places itself in the service of liturgical rites and conse-

[6] This is amplified in the *Instructio* of June 30th, five years later: "Our hope is that such art will never be admitted into our churches, still more that it may not be called upon to build those churches or to renovate or decorate them." This severity is toned down in the same document, where we read on with a sense of encouragement: "But let us open our doors, and let us reserve the most sincere welcome to every just and progressive development of the good and venerable traditions which have given proof of their inexhaustible capacity, when studied under the double light of genius and faith, to inspire new and beautiful forms."

crated edifices with the honour which is owing to them."

What all this amounts to, then, is this: let the moderns go ahead with their work, but let them show an acute consciousness of the reverence due to God and to the house of God. For Christian sculptors and painters the only aesthetic is the Christian aesthetic, and if this conflicts with the prevailing fashion there must be no concessions made. All that the Church has said in the past twenty years about art is only an expansion of what Pius X had said about it in his time: "One must not find anything in the temple which would trouble or even diminish the piety and devotion of the faithful, nothing that would give just cause for scandal, nothing unworthy of a house of prayer or of the majesty of God." So much for the theory, now for the practice.

Taking our terms from the quoted excerpts, we ask first of all what is "arid" artistic expression? In their eagerness to avoid sentiment, some of the best modern sculptors in the Church are suppressing the human element almost entirely. They are repeating the Byzantine mistake of making saints generic rather than specific. There is almost a standardized face for our Lord, and his mother differs in different statues only in the details of her dress. In laudably reducing the too personal element which was allowed in nineteenth-century carving, the sculptors of the twentieth century have arrived at the same mistake from the opposite direction. By becoming excessively mannered they have become very personal indeed, but in another way.

The Christian sculptor who exercises his talent in Christ has to guard against too abstract a treatment of human forms. The sacred humanity should never be far from the mind of the man who works his craft as a Christian. Implicit in every statue that is carved in the name of religion is the Incarnation. To dehumanize beyond a certain point may be to dechristianize as well. Future historians of Christian sculpture may well be found to praise the present mood of detachment from emotion in certain schools, but perhaps they will also see there a secularization.

Thus in "spiritualizing" sculpture there is the danger of sterilizing its Christian inspiration. The Christian character of a work does not depend upon what you take away from it but upon what you put into it. By a kind of sculptural irony the carvings that are forced artificially into an over-simplified spiritual expression end up by being more emotional than the emotional examples which they have set out to replace. Only it is an *arid* emotion, unproductive both religiously and sculpturally.

If in modern Catholic sculpture there is much that is self-conscious, it is because we who are in the craft are too little conscious of God. Where there is little spirituality in the workman there can not be much spirituality in the work. But the workman's dispositions must be left for the final chapter; enough to note here that a self-conscious striving after a holy effect results often in the unholy. The holier the theme to be carved, the greater need not only for caution but for holiness.

From consideration of the "arid" in carving we move on to the "deformed." What the Church wants to avoid is not so much an emphatic style—the Church has encouraged, as history witnesses, emphatic styles—but the grotesque which disfigures the emphatic style. Even more harmful to sculpture than the cultivated pretty is the cultivated grotesque, and the reason for this is that while the intelligentsia will never bow to the dainty they may well bow to the deformed.

Ours is by no means the first generation to manifest the grotesque in religious sculpture. The Mannerist school was all for deformity. Catholic Spain and Germany allowed, in the name of originality, exaggerations which would be censured by the Church's formula today. But where other generations have exaggerated out of devotion, ours is the first to exaggerate from the lack of it.

It is a quite different thing where you find exaggeration in the Christian art of Abyssinia, the Congo, Uganda, Nigeria, Mexico and Peru. In these lands

Christian craftsmen have simply gone on carving in their old pre-evangelized tradition. There is all the difference between preserving a primitive form and apeing one. The interest in Negro sculpture which has held its own in Europe for a quarter of a century has a good and bad side to it. The simplification and directness of an African mask are good things to study; the snub nose and thick lips are bad things to copy. African masks were originally designed to be used in the service of religion. Indirectly, as providing an index, they can still be so used—and in the service of the Christian religion—but hardly if one happens to be a European.[7]

What the Church objects to is the canonization of the extraordinary. A cult of the fantastic for the sake of the fantastic is bound to end in trouble. The fashion can become a cause, the cause can claim its martyrs, and martyrdom can win approval from the most unlikely quarters. There exists in most of us who carve stone a certain perversity, left over from the fall of man, by which we like to think that the misshapen is, if not beautiful, at least worth championing. It can become to us, if not true, at least correct.

[7] See *Liturgical Arts*, vol. 26; 4 (1958). Articles and illustrations in this issue show how the tradition has been maintained in Catholic Africa. Particularly remarkable is the work of the Dahomey school, current examples of which reveal a grasp of sculptural principles which few European schools can better.

True religious carving should aim at serenity, dignity, recollection. Deep emotions can be suggested without the least sense of strain. The Mannerists and the Romantics may not have been the first to ignore this truth and to make for nervous tension in their carving, but they were the first to make of nervous tension a criterion. The drawback about nervous tension is that those who go in for it never know where to stop.

v

Thus far, then, we have established it as a fact that the religious statue which either shocks by its crudity or nauseates by its sweetness offends against the principles of Christian art. And then, when we look round the repository displays, we wonder why nobody is doing anything about it. It is not the crude, in England at any rate, that is the trouble; the trouble lies with the charming.

The term "holy picture" means something quite different today from what it meant when holy pictures, icons, were first painted. A "holy statue" is taken to be one which looks sentimental and which expects you to be sentimental about it in return. A "holy shrine" or "devotional altar"—whether in a church, convent, private house, or garden—is not expected to affect your religion; it is expected to affect your religiosity.

This means that the whole focus has changed. Art is

no longer the handmaid to theology and the liturgy; it is the handmaid to the feelings. Theology is left to the text-book; the liturgy is left to the choir. Art is brought in to make these things less boring.

"Let the faithful have the kind of art they want" is a much repeated cry; "and if they can pray better in front of bad statues than in front of good ones, it only proves that the so-called good ones are not much use after all. Give them the bad and let them get on with it." But what the faithful want is not, in this matter of sculpture, the whole story; far the more important part of the story is what God wants. And if God wants good statues in his churches rather than bad ones he must be given them.

Bad sculpture does no service to God. It may satisfy the greater number at the lower level of taste, but it cannot of itself minister to the greater glory of God. Sculpture has not been invented to make people feel comfortable. Good sculpture, on the other hand, bears witness to the truth. It vouches for the tradition, the culture, the philosophy, from which it springs. The truth of God matters more than the feelings of man, and it is one of the functions of art to help the whole of man—not his superficial emotions merely—in the direction of truth.

Closely linked with the sensible devotion fallacy is the fallacy of intelligibility: "Give us a sculpture that *means* something." When the cry to be presented with a statuary which all can understand has been examined, it will be found to be a request for something that will tell a story. Sculpture has a more important part to play than that of *raconteur*. If we look back, we see that all periods of Christian sculpture have meant something, even if it was something which was not immediately understood. Christian sculpture of the present day, however obscure the message which some of it may bring, means something. The truth of it is that the generality of the faithful, whatever the period, want sculpture to mean what they mean. It would be more humble if they wanted it to mean what God means.

vi

After a glance round the churches, chapels, and repositories, the critical eye wanders over the studios and workshops. It might see worse, but it has, in the course of Christian history, seen better. Though some of the greatest figures in the world of sculpture today —men like Manzu, Marino Marini, Paolozzi, Giacometti, and even Picasso—derive from the Catholic culture and tradition, few could be claimed to have contributed to professedly Catholic art.[8] Certainly not

[8] Manzu has modelled several *Crucifixions* and *Depositions*, and one panel representing Saint Teresa of Lisieux.

all among those just mentioned could be said to fulfil the requirements outlined in the *Instructio*.

So when it comes to naming eminent sculptors whose work appears in Catholic churches, and who in all respects are found to meet the Holy Office's conditions, the list is small. Nor do the English figure among the best known. There are the great veteran sculptors of the century, Ivan Mestrovic and Ernst Barlach, and after these a gap. The Catholic tradition is supported by the truly religious work in stone, wood, bronze, and other materials by such considerable artists as Marc Macken, Joseph Jaekel, Jean Charlot, Lambert Rucki. With more local reputations but working in the same authentic spirit are Marc Hénard, Burch Korrodi, Marek Szwark. There must be a number of names which could be added to those given here, but one does not seem to come across them. Reproductions of the work of some new Catholic sculptor appear in art journals, and one feels that someone important is coming along, but either because the critics turn out to be harsh, or the dealers extortionate, or the public niggardly—or because the sculptor himself turns out to be venal or pusillanimous or a lover of fashion—one hears no more.

Meanwhile nothing very much is going on in England. There is no endemic Catholic carving. The nearest thing to a school of Catholic carving is the legacy left behind by Gill. If Gill had been a consistently great sculptor, this legacy might have been drawn upon with greater profit. But though he was a great leader, a great worker, a great calligrapher in stone, Gill was not always a great sculptor. While some of Gill's work— *Mankind,* for example, and the *Prospero and Ariel* group already alluded to—approaches the top rank, much of it is commonplace and a lot of it is vulgar almost to obscenity. It was his doctrine rather than his execution that influenced his generation of sculptors for good. The moment he forgot about his theory, whether in carving or in writing (for his *Autobiography* is a disagreeable and regrettable book), Gill seemed to fall apart. As a craftsman there was nobody to touch him, but if we are looking for spirituality in Catholic carving we shall not find it in Eric Gill.

Nevertheless it is highly indicative that the most significant religious sculptures to have appeared in this country since Gill's death have come from the hands of either non-Catholics or foreigners. Gill evidently gave us something which we have already lost. Henry Moore's stone *Madonna and Child* in St. Matthew's, Northampton, and Jacob Epstein's bronze *Madonna and Child* in Cavendish Square show more inspiration than the work of all our Catholic sculptors put together.

The only Catholic to have made a name for himself, and deservedly, is the expatriate Pole, Adam Kossowski, whose ceramics are truly religious in feeling and truly sculptural in form. Catholic painters and cutters of lettering[9] are plentiful enough, but there are all too few sculptors. There are indeed Englishmen who are able in their handling of stone and wood—for example, Lindsey Clark, Peter Watts, Julian Alan, and, more versatile and accomplished than any of them, Arthur Pollen—but there is today no living English Catholic tradition such as there has been in other periods. If David Jones had followed up his early experiments in three-dimensional work, and not concentrated exclusively on two, a continuity might have been preserved. But now it looks as though we in England must wait for a quite new inspiration. One thing is certain: that when such an inspiration comes, if it comes at all, it will not be recognized for what it is.

So while foreigners in this country are exploring with great success the sculptural possibilities of concrete,

[9] Painting is outside the range of this book, but the cutting of inscriptions is no mean part of sculpture. Dom Basil Robinson, monk of Prinknash now working at the dependent house at Pluscarden, is probably the most finished performer in this field. The Prinknash school of pottery and the crafts carried on at St. Michael's, Farnborough, owe much to Dom Basil's inspiration. Both Prinknash and Farnborough have produced modelled figures for reproduction in plaster. The lettering on the west wall of the pavilion at Downside, commemorating the death of those killed in an aeroplane accident, was cut by Dom Basil Robinson.

aluminium, brick, tin, zinc, compressed and glazed pulp, we English who belong to the faith which inspired the splendid idiom of the Romanesque and the creative enterprise of the Gothic are still slogging away at the old materials and turning out the old familiar shapes. "Sculpture in England is without imagination and direction," says Epstein. This, when understood in relation to religious work, points to the most melancholy conclusions. Is it only in our own age and in our own country that the faith which we hold is not strong enough to provide us with these two things, imagination and direction?

vii

The findings of the present chapter can now be summarized. Assuming that the conclusions are agreed upon, it can be claimed that sacred sculpture can develop only under certain conditions. Of these the primary condition is collaboration between the Church and the craft. Each member in this relationship is to respect certain norms. Thus if the faithful are expected to behave themselves in church, so also are carvings. Again, if sculptors are expected to assume expert religious knowledge in their clergy, the clergy for their part are expected to assume a professional knowledge in those among their congregations who happen to be sculptors.

In the concessions to be made by either side, the weight would seem to be pretty evenly divided. The clergy have a right to demand that the carvings which occupy their church-space are possessed of the power to please others besides the initiated. But at the same time the clergy must remember the words of a great Catholic artist, Severini, who says that it is not easy to appreciate a work of art "if between it and its appreciation there stands a screen of insufficient culture." To justify its title as a work of Christian art, a carving does not have to be understood by all or liked by all. The sculptor claims no more than that the work which has faithfully obeyed the canons, both of sculpture and the Christian aesthetic, will move the *unprejudiced* beholder to pleasure, edification, and (if the beholder plays his part) to prayer.

Accordingly (and this is the point which has to be recalled by the clergy, the faithful, the professionals), the test lies not in what the expert critic thinks about the carving, nor yet in what the devout beholder thinks about it if he is approaching it with preconceived ideas about the identification of art with nature, but rather in the response which it elicits from those who bring to it an open mind. It is only the open mind which can read the symbols—guessing at them at first but becoming accustomed to the language—of a science which necessarily possesses its own terminology.

Sculpture has no reason to be resentful of the Church's attitude. The Church has the duty, at this time especially, of being on its guard. In the confusion of ideologies, each eventually bringing to the surface its own appropriate expression, the Church can take no risks. Artistic expressions must be held up steadily and long before the light of truth, and sculpture should not wish it otherwise. Contemporary sculpture should know that if it is true, its truth will assert itself and receive the Church's favour; if it is not true, it is of no consequence and the sooner it perishes the better.

History has shown that in those periods when civilization seemed most confused, and when art was at its lowest ebb, the authentic spirit was only waiting to declare itself. "There must be chaos that out of chaos may come forth new stars," wrote Nietzsche, echoing the voice of the Hebrew prophets. Perhaps the chaotic state of modern art, secular particularly but religious also, is the prelude to another great resurgence such as Christian centuries have witnessed in the past.

Certain it is that the muddle of current sculptural fashions which go to make up what is called (imprecisely, because all styles have been that) the "contemporary style" could not have been manifested in any other age than our own. Whether the purer elements commanded by twentieth-century sculpture prevail, leaving permanent record of our aspirations, or whether fervid eclecticism will go on winning, leaving nothing behind but rubble, remains a matter for the sculptors themselves to decide. And since it is now up to the carvers and modellers, it will be their attitude rather than anyone else's which must constitute the subject-matter of the next and final chapter.

5. *Immediate*

i

THE most immediate approach to stone-carving is the stone-carver's. It will be this approach that we shall consider in these concluding sections. What follows is simply an attempt to prove that a man makes images of what he is primarily searching for, and that his work is therefore shaped by the end to which he puts it.

So by the roundabout way which has been adopted —taking in history, theory, and the different means by which carving is evaluated—we come back to the work itself and to the mind of the man responsible for it. In such an arrangement there is bound to be a certain amount of repetition, but since this seemed to be the best arrangement for the development of the idea, the repetition cannot be helped.

Now it is obvious that the conditions which govern the inwardness of sculpture will be at once more subtle and less easy to prove than those which govern its outwardness. But though the qualities now insisted upon cannot be referred for measurement to objective standards, the existence of those qualities must be as-

sumed of the kind of sculpture which we are particularly considering.

In the approach to Christian sculpture from the
inside, as one who shapes religious objects which are
designed to minister to the glory of God and to the
religious sense of the faithful, a man proposes to himself a twofold ideal: that of perfecting his craft and
that of perfecting his Christian spirit. To the degree
that he is faithful in the pursuit of this twofold purpose
he arrives at unity of achievement and unity of soul.
His work is part of himself and he is part of his work.

When a man's conscience as a craftsman is informed
and directed by his conscience as a Christian, the
activity is no longer divided, and the works which he
produces will be truly religious. "Every artist knows
that the form of the statue is not the outside of the
statue," says Chesterton, "but rather the inside of the
statue; even in the sense of the inside of the sculptor."

The shape of a statue is a matter of surface; the form
of a statue is a matter of essence. Form has come to
mean shape, but it much more truly means idea, conception, intimation, individual being or entity. A machine can give to a statue its shape but it cannot—
except in the sense that such a statue would be formally
and fundamentally a machine-made article—give to a
statue its form. Form—as in the case of statues, so in
the case of men—has to do with the mind.

But when all this high-sounding stuff has been said,

the fact remains that sculpture as we see it is the result of someone's hacking at a lump of stone. So, working from the outward to the inward, it will be this manual side of the business which we shall consider, in the context of explicitly Christian craftsmanship, before we move on to consider the intellectual and spiritual sides.

ii

The block of stone which has been casually and carelessly shaped will bring neither praise to God nor assistance to the faithful in their worship. A work may have a religious direction and destination, but if it lacks conscientious execution it cannot qualify as a work of Christian art. The sculptor who is true only to his religious aspiration and not to the principles of his craft may produce works of interest, and even of edification, but these will not be works of Christian art.

The sculptor's responsibility towards the technique of sculpture will not be satisfied until certain primary demands—demands which to some might seem elementary—are met. If he is to carve properly, the sculptor may never lose sight of his drawing, his anatomy, his structure, his composition. It may be boring to have to go on studying these things, but sculpture is very hard work, and hard work can be excessively boring.

Immediate

Drawing is to the sculptor what steps are to the
dancer and notes are to the musician. For a sculptor
to claim that his business is to make shapes, and that
therefore he can neglect lines and the variations suggested by lines, would be as mistaken as for an actor
to claim that since his business is to act he can neglect
articulation and the various inflections suggested in
articulation. The sculptor may not mumble in his
sculpture.

So Rodin's definition of sculpture as "un dessein de
toutes les côtés," which does *not* mean an everlasting
profile, must remain a basic principle. Only when the
implications of this definition have been worked out
will the carving assume the quality of solid and "designed" sculpture.[1] That the definition did not mean
for Rodin the sacrifice of the substantial to the linear

[1] "To Maillol in his preoccupation with the problem of
achieving the maximum *roundness* of form, Rodin's conception
of sculpture as 'the art of the hump and the hollow' was wholly
unacceptable; only the 'blonde shadow,' the shadow that is
not accentuated by a hollow, being permissible in his eyes. As
Maurice Denis put it in words which typify Maillol's ideal:
'To achieve beauty of form, the modelling must be rounded
and without depressions,' since beauty of form is built up by
means of smooth rounded surfaces."—E. H. Ramsden, *Sculpture: Theme and Variations*, p. 22. It is significant in this connection that the *Three Fates* of the Parthenon, which Maillol
would probably not have looked at twice, was the carving admired by Rodin beyond any other.

is seen from the works themselves which he produced, and which in the words of Eugène Carrière "emerge from the earth and return to it, like giant boulders, the rocks and dolmens of primeval solitude." Rodin himself tells how as an apprentice he learned from a certain Simon "never to think of a surface except as the extremity of a volume."

While there is no substitute in sculpture for volume, nothing but careful drawing can express it. Having to think of one's drawing when one wants above all to rush on with the modelling is a great nuisance. One knows that enthusiasm is a wasting asset, and that too much drawing may hold things up and drain one's zest. Nevertheless if one gets ahead of the drawing, giving impulse a free rein, one loses direction and the composition becomes indeterminate, sloppy. It is drawing that ties the whole thing together and acts as a check on the chisel. You might think that without the cramping discipline of drawing, the work would achieve greater spontaneity. In fact the reverse seems to be true: the asceticism imposed by drawing is found to bring out more clearly and directly from the stone whatever it is of beauty that the artist has seen.

But drawing does more than curb the impetuosity of the artist; it develops the sensibility of the artist. Whether he is a painter or a sculptor, he learns through his drawing to see clearly before he starts to work out on the material in front of him, and therefore in a new idiom, the things which he sees. If Rouault, bringing to paint the line and feel of stained glass, were to lose touch with the drawing, his compositions would be no more than decorative patterns.

Equally tedious to the eager performer is the study of anatomy. But if a doctor cannot afford to forget the skeleton, nor can the sculptor. In order to express any part of the human body in stone, it is not enough to think only of the flesh surfaces. It is the bone structure which makes the first call upon one's attention. Anyone who examines the work in bronze of Dora Gordine or of Jacob Epstein will see at once what is meant here. Where Dora Gordine goes in for smooth rounded modelling, Epstein chooses to break up his surfaces and to make the most of hollows; but though very different in finish there is the same feeling, in each artist, for the firmness which is given by the bones underneath.

To be scornful of the anatomical aspect of the carved figure is to risk affectation. It also leads to sheer bad craftsmanship. A carved hand which looks well enough when seen from the front, when seen from the side turns into a foot. Granted that stone hands are not meant to be replicas of human hands, they are meant to possess a constituent affinity. Anyway they are not meant to look like feet.

So until a man can carve without having to think

where the bones and muscles go—and can anyone carve with such sureness?—the sculptor will be obliged to refer to the actual formation of the body. Particularly is this necessary where the figure is hidden under folds of drapery; an arm or a leg can, in the stylized treatment of stiff materials, get lost in the clothes which cover it. Rodin is said to have modelled the six figures of his *Burghers of Calais* first without clothes, and only when he was sure that he had got this right did he add the dress in which the group finally appeared.

Directly connected with the above, but extending over a wider range, is the question of structure. If carving is to be expressed solidly, it must be expressed structurally. Carved decoration in churches shows sometimes an astonishing unconcern with the structure of ordinary common objects—let alone that of important objects. A bunch of grapes, a sheaf of wheat, a chalice, the instruments of the Passion: there is a proper structure to every object and even to every symbol. It is a mistake to think of structure only in connection with blocks of flats, pylons, and suspension bridges.

Anyone who has tried to carve the stations of the cross will know the tendency on the part of spears and planks to wrap themselves round whatever lies immediately behind. These things seem to roll as though made of plasticine. It means that construction has been overlooked. The outline of the drawing may have been preserved, but the significance of the drawing has been lost: the drawing has had nothing to hang on to, and the carving has got into difficulties.

The fourth point to be considered here is that of composition. What Belloc said of literary composition might equally be said of sculptural composition: "Everything must look the same way." Neither styles nor techniques may be mixed in the one carving, and unless the minor features are related to the dominant theme there will be a division of interest and a lack of direction. While composition depends mostly upon what is done before the work of carving begins, it depends also upon what can happen when the work is under way. If the sculptor allows himself no margin of change, keeping to the original plan within an eighth of an inch, he may well see his composition stiffen under his hand. If, at the other extreme, he pays little attention to the design which he has worked out, he is taking the risk of de-composition.

It would probably be the experience of most sculptors that when working in the round the tendency is towards over-simplification, and when working in relief the tendency is towards the opposite. There are fewer flat planes on a statue, tempting the admission of decoration. It is never easy to judge how much detail to allow, but certainly in the case of carving reliefs the detail must be kept well under control. In a panel there are likely to be awkward spaces crying out to be filled, awkward corners limiting the freedom of the bodies, awkward and artificial boundaries which are either difficult to reach or else impossible to extend.

While working in the round provides problems of composition—how to balance the masses, allow for the play of light and shade, distribute the interest, present the thing as a unified whole—working in relief provides the same problems with a few more added. In a relief, for example, the perspectives cannot be shown by straightforward head-on cutting as they can be shown in the case of cutting statues in the round. Working more or less on the flat, the carver has to indicate, by oblique cutting and sometimes by undercutting, a sense of depth. Since the depth is not there it has to be suggested, contrived.[2] Contrary to the layman's expectation, a relief is harder to bring off sucessfully than a full statue in the round. *Rima* was a greater challenge to Sir Jacob Epstein's genius than *Night*.

The temptation to pack a relief tight with detail is

[2] See plate XI, which shows Blessed Oliver Plunkett's nose, because of the three-quarter profile of the head, set at an exaggerated angle. Where this sort of thing is well done, the exaggeration of the angle is not noticed. Here the angle is noticed at once.

one which almost all schools, at one time or another in their history, have yielded to. The Greeks, the Romans, and even the carvers of the Romanesque have overcrowded. Less guilty were the Egyptians and the two Mesopotamian civilizations. It is curious to note that in our own time, when film companies vie with one another in the number of human beings whom they can show upon the screen at once, there should be a return to the spacious panels of Babylon and the shallow reliefs to be found in the tombs and temples which watched beside the waters of the Nile. It is gratifying to think that it is sculpture which, for all its faults, has chosen to proceed in inverse relation to modern forms of visual entertainment. Few of the other arts could boast the same.

iii

If the four points considered in the preceding section correspond, by the demand which they make of the sculptor, to Christian patience and restraint, the points to be considered now correspond to Christian humility. Humility is not a virtue which is much associated with sculptors, but is nevertheless more needed by them than by members of most other professions. Had it not been for the Renaissance and its effect upon art, the need might not have been so marked; but with the Renaissance came publicity. Hitherto it was the work that mattered, not the prestige that would follow the work. Prestige went to the artist's head, and he has been suffering from it ever since.

This is not a plea for the return of the carver to his pre-Renaissance anonymity, which in any case would be economically impossible, but rather for his acknowledgement of pre-Renaissance religious and social status. The carver is a Christian manual workman. He has got above himself, and his work—as always happens when a man lives beyond his station—shows it. Just because sculpture has something important to say, it must beware of rhetoric, grandiloquence, didacticism.

Still more is this a plea for the shedding of other elements than those of naturalism, gallery-play, and virtuosity which the Renaissance introduced; the most important thing to be shed is self. The responsibility is now no longer technical but moral. Thus before our modern and often much simplified sculpture—simplified to excellent effect—can recapture the purity of the early Christian work which we have considered in the historical section of this book, it will have to care less about self-expression and more about the expression of religion.

So long as a work of sculpture is thought of as an interesting expression of an interesting personality it is hindered from performing its true function in the

Christian scheme. The fault is partly the layman's for advancing the workman to a rank for which he is unsuited, but this does not absolve the workman from eager complicity. Particularly in this mass-producing age of ours we delight in being able to stand out, by reason of our special gift, from the common herd.

The stone-cutter, moreover, in virtue of his Christian humility, must submit not only, as we have seen, to the Church but also to the Church's tradition. While granting that there is no fixed pattern of orthodoxy in Christian sculpture—since tradition does not sit still while you bring along your contemporary exhibits for a judgment upon their orthodoxy—contemporary sculpture should be humble enough to know that the frankly *un*orthodox is an offence against the faithful, against authority, against God. It does a disservice too, in the long run, to sculpture itself.

This does not mean that in any one school of modern sculpture there must be evidence of the early cultures —as though we could combine the power of the Assyrians, the cool dignity of the Egyptians, the roundness of Buddhist carving as it is to be found particularly in China, the rhythm and lightness of the dancing figures of India, the line and grace of Greece, the majestic urbanity of Rome, the composition and spirituality of the Byzantines, the sculptural directness of the Romanesque, the feeling of the early Gothic, the *Gewandtheit* of the Renaissance and the contrivance of the Baroque—because this would lead to utter confusion. The school that sets out to be a pantheon ends up as a junk-shop. What is wanted is not an assortment of styles but a respect for style. Without a respect for Christian and pre-Christian traditions in sculpture, a workman would be in danger of cutting himself off from a channel of inspiration. The aesthetic pleasure to be derived from the sight of carvings which belong to cultures earlier than our own is not the only reason for looking at historical works of art. As good a reason is to provide a frame, but a flexible frame, of reference.

Tradition, like nature, is to the sculptor the background against which he works. It does not determine his manner, which is an individual thing, but it probably conditions his having a manner at all. Very few sculptors, however creative, can work entirely out of their heads. Even those who think that they work entirely from their own reserves are in fact drawing upon the law of sculptural heredity. Anyway if they repudiate an ancestry, sculptors will produce only ill-bred, vulgar work.

If humility is needed for judging other people's work, it is needed even more in judging one's own. Hand in hand with any sort of carving, but especially with religious carving, must go self-criticism. The sculptor should not be above saying, as he stands back to look at his work, "This does not suggest piety, it suggests coyness; and heaven defend us from the coy." He should not be above saying: "I have wanted to express nobility and instead have expressed pomposity; it cannot go at that." The humble sculptor does not confuse the grand with the grandiose or the tender with the insipid; he is detached enough, spiritually, to see the work as it really is.

So it is only the humble man who can fully understand his own work. The proud man is blinded by self-deception and sees only what he wants to see. The proud man's mistakes are hidden from him, are excused, are rationalized. The proud man can analyse everyone else's work but his own. He can go on for years making shapes, even technically well-finished shapes (if his criticism can extend to technique), but if he does not understand them, or understands them wrong, the things which he makes are not truly religious. Pride is the negation of the religious spirit, and if the religious spirit is denied in the man, it will be denied to the work which he performs.

So we are back again at the principle that the *form* of the work is given by the thought processes that are going on in the man who, for better or worse, shapes the thing. In this connection Mr. Ramsden, in the book frequently referred to in these pages, quotes Brancusi as saying that "les choses ne sont pas difficiles à faire, mais nous de nous mettre en état de les faire."[3] This is a profound observation, summing up much of what has been treated already and what remains yet to be treated. To it Mr. Ramsden in a footnote adds aptly that "those who so lightly dismiss work which they do not understand, might do well to remember concurrently that 'les choses ne sont pas difficiles a *comprendre,* mais nous de nous mettre en état de les comprendre.' "[4]

Unless the sculptor puts himself in the disposition for making, and *unless* the spectator puts himself in the disposition for understanding, there is bound to be a breakdown in communication. "The more closely a work of art is attuned to truth," says Severini, "the more aggressive it may, and often does, appear. An authentic work of art is often apparently hostile and unappealing . . . but the more sincerely we attempt to penetrate it, to realize the special importance of the subject and its intrinsic character, the more it becomes possible eventually to appreciate even the intrinsic side of the work, for everything is correlated."[5]

[3] *Sculpture: Theme and Variations,* p. 43.

[4] "An index to the philosophy of art in which Brancusi became increasingly absorbed lies in the recognition that he combines, at once and in a superlative degree, the ideal of the artist as workman and the artist as seer."—*Ibid.*

[5] "Modern Artist and Sacred Art," an article in *Modern Sacred Art* (Sands, 1938).

Lastly the stone-cutter must be humble, as well as charitable, in the allowances which he makes for the non-comprehension of others. Arrogance in the cause of good taste is no better than arrogance in the cause of bad taste. The fact that to me it appears abundantly clear that ignorance and prejudice are at the back of the violence with which inferior art is defended does not give me the right to claim personal superiority. What is not so clear to me is that behind my own championship of true art there may lie a cultural snobbery which does more harm than the false art which I am attacking.

To conclude. The Christian sculptor subordinates himself and his work to Christ. However successful he may be in mastering his craft, he submits to being mastered by the principles of the Gospel. Nor is this a question merely of giving interior assent to a doctrine; it is a question also of giving exterior obedience to a Church. This means that intellectually he thinks in a Christian way, morally he behaves in a Christian way, artistically he carves in a Christian way. Such is the workman's logical approach to religious carving, religious living, religious believing.

iv

The subjects now to be treated relate in one way or another to the Christian sculptor's integrity. As a functioning member of Christ's mystical body the workman must show in his attitude towards his craft that he has taken his stand on truth. If his works belie his principles, they are bad works and he is a bad workman. He may not—whatever the inducements from others, whether the particular pressure is devotional, economic, or of current fashion—deliver what he knows to be bad sculpture. To justify such action would be the same as to justify lying.

It is significant that the word "sincerity" was given to the language by sculpture. When the Romans, eager to follow the Greeks in all things cultural, started to carve in marble they were not always successful. The mistakes which they made in the cutting were covered up by the application of a wax which exactly matched the colour of the marble, so that when a carving was produced which had needed nothing to hide the flaws it was pronounced *sine cera*. If the Romans discovered eventually that it was easier to produce statues than sculptors *sine cera*, then there is all the more reason why Christian sculptors should make sincerity their business.

We saw in the first chapter how sculpture must be true to the material chosen for the work: an extrinsic relationship. We come now to see how it must be true to the purpose chosen for the work: an intrinsic relationship. The merit of a piece of Christian carving, in other words, must be judged by direct and not indirect standards.

To know the number of slaves employed on the job does not affect the essential significance of the pyramids. To speculate on how many craftsmen must have died from working underground is not to say that the murals in the tomb of Tutankhamen are either good or bad. To state how long it took to hew Petra out of its native rock, how long it took to build the west front at Chartres, how long it took to complete the Franco memorial to the dead of the Spanish civil war (with its subterranean granite chapel 285 feet long and hollowed out of a Guadamarra mountain), or again how *short* a time it took to put up the United Nations building in New York: none of this is to tell anything of artistic merit or demerit.

Thus a man may not say: "Here is a carved presentation of the Grotto at Lourdes: I scooped it out with nothing but a shoehorn given to me by the Bishop"; nor may he say "This model of St. Patrick's Cathedral is made entirely of candle-ends collected from its own sacristy." So far as it concerns sculpture the man may have carved the grotto with his teeth and the cathedral in cheese. Where the appeal is made in terms extraneous to the nature of the work it is made under false pretences.

It is accordingly to apply false standards of valuation when a carving is judged by the price paid for it, the sacrifices entailed in securing it, the risks run in transporting it, the reputation acquired by possessing it. Partly responsible for such false standards are guidebooks and travel-agents' catalogues; partly responsible also are patrons who boast about how much they have subscribed, dealers who raise what they inaccurately call the value of the work, the newspapers which shape their reader's minds, and such public bodies as arts committees, memorial funds, parish councils and church decorating societies which are forever either making appeals or publishing statistics. Partly responsible too are the sculptors themselves.

If considerations extrinsic to the work's essential character may not weigh, what happens when it is clear that the essential character has been profoundly influenced by circumstances which have nothing to do with sculpture? For example, a personal sorrow may be the cause of a particular carving being what it is. May not the work be judged indirectly, by dwelling upon the qualities which went into it? If a work depends upon the thought of the one who expresses it, is not the supposed emotional background of the work as good a guide as any?

But if you allow that his integrity prevents a sculptor from making a bid for approval by pointing to outside contingencies such as those outlined above, you must allow that it forbids him equally, indeed all the more, to win sympathy on purely personal grounds. It would be just as contrary to the idea of integrity for a sculptor to acquire a name for himself by letting his stone-work look as though it had come to the surface through a sea of heart-blood and warm tears as for a painter to get a name for himself with his murals by using for pigment only tomato sauce and warm tar.

On the other hand, the fact has to be taken into account that because a man's talent is to a certain extent moulded by his emotional and religious and intellectual experience, influences which reflect these experiences will appear in his work. Such influences are not accidental but substantial: the evidence which they give is intrinsic to the carving, not merely to the carver.

Suffering, as deepening his character and heightening his sensitivity, can undoubtedly play a large part in a sculptor's interpretation of his theme. A fairly confident guess might be made, for example, that Rodin had known suffering from the inside. The same guess might be made of Barlach, Lehmbruck, Kollwitz, and any number of others. It is possible that out of some great sorrow the crowning touch of genius emerges. Be this as it may, it should not be sorrow *as such* that the sculptor must try to express; he must try to express truth and beauty according to the principles of the medium which he uses.

Nor is it sorrow *as such*, accordingly, that the spectator must look for when he is trying to make up his mind about a work. Where the subject is intended to suggest sorrow, as in scenes from the Passion, it is another matter altogether. Here it is not the sculptor's sorrow that is in question, but Christ's and humanity's. The sculptor's sorrows must be kept out of it.

Since the recognition of what sculpture is all about depends upon the relation of three entities—the sculptor, the spectator, the work—each of the three entities must be functioning at its essential level. The emotions, however powerful, are not strictly of the essence in the case of any of them. Thus for a work to gain credit for the tragedy which is suspected to be lying behind it—a tragedy which is the workman's domestic concern and which has no direct bearing upon the object carved—is to make itself a victim of the anguish fallacy.

Certainly for a sculptor to make capital out of a private grief would be highly reprehensible. The tensions which he endures within himself are meant to be resolved in faith and not conveyed in stone. "The believing artist lives in a great solitude," says Severini, who goes on to show how the artist more than any is the victim of our modern materialistic society.[6] The contradictions are such that the sculptor is harder hit, inwardly and perhaps outwardly, than the man who employs him. At least so Severini thinks. But we sculp-

[6] *Op. cit.*, p. 100.

tors as a tribe are a self-pitying lot, so it does not do to
dwell too much upon this aspect of our calling.

As easy to detect in carving, though hardly less mis-
leading than the other, is the note of joy. This is just
as well, or it might be thought that the bulk of Christian carving has shown itself to be sad. Examples of
cheerful carving can be found in the normally imper-
sonal reliefs of the Romanesque tradition. If there was
cheerful carving and iconography in the Byzantine
schools, it does not much appear. The Gothic tradition is full of it.[7] The same gaiety can be traced through
the Renaissance,[8] Baroque,[9] and later schools down to
the present day[10] What all this is leading up to is that
though the note of joy is one to be expected of Christian sculpture, it is not a note which rings infallibly of
truth and beauty. There must be qualities more funda-

[7] Typical is the *Madonna and Child* at Nüremburg, believed
to have been carved by Veit Stoss in about 1500.

[8] Typical is *The Boy with a Dolphin* by Verrocchio, and the
countless *Putti* in bronze and ceramic.

[9] Typical are Bernini's angels, the *Solomon Pillar* of St.
Bento, Oporto, and, a little later, Falconnet's *Cupid,* which is
frankly Rococo.

[10] Not so typical of the present-day trend in Christian sculpture, but typical in the sense that it reveals the nature of the
man who produces it, is the work of Carl Milles, whose powerful masses and severe lines are lightened by a gentle mockery.
Milles, not a Catholic, is surely one of the most important
sculptors of our time.

mental than joy to indicate truth and beauty; joy is a by-product.

Since it is the sculptor's job to "make out of stone" (the definition is Gill's) "things seen in the mind,"[11] it follows that the mind which sees things sadly will express itself in carving things sadly, the mind which sees things happily will carve in a happy way. *Actio sequitur esse.* But it is the Christian sculptor's especial job to "make out of stone" symbols of the fundamental. That is his first duty. Whether he makes them happily or unhappily is his own private affair. It is his sincerity as an artist which will tell him what concessions he can afford to make to his mood and habit of mind.

Connected with this idea of integrity, though more as a refinement than as an integral part of it, is the question of how far external help may be employed in the carving. If new instruments for cutting stone are invented, they can obviously be put to use. Stone-cutters since prehistoric times have been trying out new tools and perfecting their equipment. But there can come a point at which the equipment does all the work while the sculptor sits back and directs. If he is to preserve his identity as a workman, a cutter of stone, a carver, the man must operate at first hand; there must be something in the exercise which engages his fingers as well as his brain. If an electric cutter enables

[11] *Op. cit.,* p. 21.

him to get a finer line or smoother edge than anything which he would be able to get with the chisel, let him use it. But to do the whole thing by machinery would seem a too radical delegation. If you happen to be carving the heads of the Presidents of the United States on the side of a mountain, you must presumably use a system of drills more or less remotely controlled, because there does not appear to be any other way of doing it. But fortunately the occasion very seldom arises.

"If we are going to be stone-carvers, then we must be both craftsmen and designers," says Eric Gill, "and if that combination is impossible then stone-carving is, as an occupation worthy of free men, non-existent and we must find another trade."[12] Here it is a question not of getting a machine but of getting another man to take part in the enterprise. Christian sculpture should arise out of the mind of the executant, and if it does not do this there is a loss of unity, of integrity. Conceived by a mind other than the executant's, and taking shape only under the executant's chisels, the work is a short step from being a factory product.

The sculptor Thorwaldsen, a leading exponent of Neo-Classicism in the early nineteenth century, used to have the main work carried out by assistants; all he did was to come in towards the end and finish it

[12] *Sculpture*, p. 35.

off.[13] Canova, who was also a Neo-Classicist of the same period, worked in a quite different way. Canova's sculptural integrity was such that he not only did every inch of the work himself but insisted that his apprentices, who had been required to do a year's novitiate in a stone quarry in order to get the feel of the material, should themselves do every inch of their own work without help from himself or from one another. It was again a sign of his rigid adherence to principle that Canova carved his figures exactly to the measurements of the models who sat for him. After all that, it is curious to find how boring orthodox, official, classical beauty can be.

The case of modelling, as distinct from carving, is not quite the same. Here the sculptor feels free (apparently) to turn over to another for casting the first fruit of his design. He has handled the clay himself, and he regards the work of casting as a separate art-form. This is a recognized convention. Henry Moore, Picasso, and a number of leading modern sculptors get a man in Paris to do their casting for them. It seems he does it very well. But it makes the analogy of creation take a curious turn.

[13] Ramsden (*op. cit.*, p. 7) relates how the Prince of Bavaria, knowing this habit of Thorwaldsen's, made it a condition when he commissioned the carving of the *Adonis* that the master should handle the work from start to finish.

This point about producing one's own work can best be seen the other way round: what happens when one produces other people's? Work done to another man's blueprint will inevitably lack something of the creative impulse which gives the thing life. There are good excuses on both sides: the workman may be doing it as the only way to earn a living; the designer may feel happy enough about drawing what he wants, but less happy about being able to make anything come out of his drawing.

So for a creative work of sculpture there have to be continuity and unity. Just as the actor should want to do his own make-up, and as the author should want to write his own footnotes and draw up his own index, so the sculptor should want to see his own composition through all its stages from the mental picture to the removal van.[14]

It is of course possible that the stone-cutter who

---

[14] I must confess to having myself transgressed in this matter: once in asking someone to provide an index to a book *(Downside By and Large)*, and on two occasions when drawings of mine were used for the carving of statues in wood. In the second case I pleaded that I worked badly in wood, and that I could find any number of deserving carvers who would do the job much better. Nevertheless I have felt since as a man would feel who said: "I never join my children at their evening prayers or kiss them goodnight; I leave it to their nanny, who does these things so much better than I do."

carries out his own designs, who does not get a hack to do the manual side of the thing for him, may so work to a formula that it comes to the same thing in the end. The continuity is snapped not by a division of operation but by routine operation. There are stone-cutters who have a pattern, in design and execution, from which they never depart. Carvings come away from their workshops having made no difference to them whatever. And they, the supposed creators, have made very little difference to the carvings. This is a kind of sculptural automation which often appears at the end of a tradition. If the day comes when the work of carving does nothing to the mind of the carver except awaken a desire to leave off when the hooter goes, then will the machine age have arrived indeed. Sculpture which has evoked no interior response from its creator cannot be expected to evoke much response from the spectator. At best such carving will look as if it had been done in sleep, at worst as if it had been done in hell.

v

The problem presenting itself as the result of the conclusion just reached is how to keep stone-work alive. The solution must lie not in the originality of the composition but in the vitality of the composer. If the stone-cutter is aware of his vocation as (to quote Brancusi's term) a "seer," and is faithful to it, he comes not only to see more of truth himself but also to show more of truth to others. His talent launches him, whether he likes it or not, on a mission. The sculptor, no less than the writer and the apostle, has the twofold duty of being vital and of coming out into the open. "Only those who are essentially alive," wrote Igor Stravinsky, "can discover real life in those who are supposedly dead." Life and truth go together.

It is not the fact that he is a Catholic that makes a sculptor dedicated: he is dedicated as a sculptor, and his Catholicism shows him the implications of this. The sculptor is trying to get nearer to truth; Catholicism is telling him where to look, and how to get there, and what it is. A Zen philosopher or a Greek pedagogue, a Kafka or a Thoreau, a Thomist or an Existentialist: all are seeing an aspect of truth, are trying to see more, are wondering how to communicate their vision to others. No man is self-sufficient, is able to live exclusively to himself.

The sculptor does not exist solely to make shapes, any shapes. He exists to make good ones—even though everyone else wants bad. And he will make good ones only to the degree that he is orientated towards truth. It should be noticed that in Gill's postulate as to the work of carving—that the sculptor must make out of stone "things seen in the mind"—it is not the visual imagination that is the first concern, but the *mind*. And again "Conceiving things in stone, and conceiving them as made by carving": the conception called for here is an intellectual and not an emotional process.

The area of investigation is accordingly narrowed: the mind apprehending truth, the hands carving things which bear witness to truth. And at this stage the Gospel comes in to reveal truth incarnate, life itself, and the certain way. The approach to Christian sculpture is defined, and the sculptor can say, "I work, now not I, but Christ worketh in me."

Without this orientation, this assured direction, the Christian sculptor will never produce truly religious work. "In order to paint the things of Christ"—these are the only recorded words of Fra Angelico—"you must think the thoughts of Christ." Lacking the thoughts of Christ, a man may carve crucifixes and crib-figures and statues of our Lady till he is too old to swing a mallet; these things may all be listed in the catalogues as objects of sacred art; they will not bear the stamp of Christ. Sculpture, with its bent for irony, seems so to arrange its laws that works of piety turn out, when not conceived in the authentic spirit, to be works of burlesque. A sculptor may call himself a Christian, may take his work seriously, and yet produce works which do not at all look serious. The reason for this is that they are not, in the true sense, Christian: they have not been carved in Christ.

vi

This brings us finally to the paramount duty of prayer. If the outward activity is to be directed effectively towards God, there must be a corresponding activity going on within. How else, if not by the light which comes to the soul in its relationship with God in prayer, can a man come to see what beauty is about? How else can he learn how best to present whatever it is of beauty that is granted him to see?

The sculptor must pray not because he loves sculpture or because he loves prayer, but because he wants to love God. Not because he wants to be a success at carving, but because he wants to be a success at serving God through carving. Learning truth in prayer, he cannot but love what he learns; loving truth, he cannot but express it in his work. And so it goes on, round and round in the ascending spiral of the full Christian life.

If people prayed more, they would be able to distinguish better between reality and unreality. Without prayer a man stays always on the level of the created world, and consequently sees only one view of it. Prayer raises him to a different level, from which he can see the created world more as God sees it. It is from this level that he begins to see created beauty as it really is, begins to see how it is related to the beauty of God.

Seeing all this, a man will still need continued prayer to keep his eyes trained upon what he sees. Otherwise he will get his vision out of focus. And if he is to convey the import of that vision to other people by his work, he will need all the more to be a man of prayer.

This is not just a piece of special pleading, a pious flourish with which to end up; it is the proposal of an ideal which alone can restore Christian sculpture to the place where it belongs. Nor is it such an airy dream that it can find no practical realization. It turns out in practice to mean that the relative values with which we are surrounded all day long are seen *as* relative: not of *no* importance or of *supreme* importance, but possessed of their own particular importance in relation to God and in the scheme of the universe.

If his work enjoys this unique significance, it is accordingly right for a sculptor to pray for the success of his work. It is right that he should want to give pleasure by his carving. Without scruple he may pray that his work will please others besides God, that it will earn money besides giving pleasure. It is only when publicity or money is the primary concern that the prayer for success is, together with the work itself, vitiated by greed.

Thus prayer is to be thought of more as giving the success to God than as trying to get it out of him. A man prays not to draw God down to his level but to raise himself to the level where God's will and his unite. In this way the emphasis becomes both more objective and more comprehensive. Understood as creating the environment of his work, the climate in which his talent best flourishes, prayer is to the sculptor the permanent background to his activity. It is not so much the prayer of the three-quarter on his knees before the game—"O Queen of heaven, only pass out the ball to the wing and I will do all the rest"—it is rather the prayer of one who is constantly directing himself and his work towards God, and who trusts that God will regulate his *ad hoc* achievement.

So it is that ideally the sculptor, like any other worker in any other field, goes beyond the notion of prayer as a particular preparation for what he has to do—as a kind of home-work which entitles him to success when the time comes—and arrives at an exercise which is performed before, during, and after the actual handling of his material. That which informs the Christian sculptor's mind by the habit of prayer flows as it were through his veins and along his arms until it communicates itself from his fingers to the chisel and from the chisel to the stone. In this way the carver becomes himself an instrument, like the instruments he uses, and there is no higher vocation than to be the ready instrument of God. Ideally the Christian sculptor prays as he carves, and carves what he prays.

Index

Index

Index

Index

Index